Praise for D.E. Paulk a

[Bishop Paulk's] preaching is as easy-going as the church's approach to differences. No wagging fingers or thunderous revelations. He treats parishioners as fellow companions on a spiritual journey. He sprinkles his conversational sermons with references to everyone from the Buddha to Teddy Pendergrass.

> **JOHN BLAKE,** *CNN Enterprise writer and producer*

Tony's writing is engaging, delightful, and thought-provoking.

> **RUBY K. PAYNE, PH.D.**, *author, A Framework for Understanding Poverty and Learning Structures*

Descended from generations of Southern preachers, [Bishop Paulk] is now a preacher himself, though a different breed…

> **KATHERINE MARSH**, *writer, "Son of a Preacher Man" in Rolling Stone Magazine*

[Dr. Burks] is one of the young geniuses engaged in the noble work of transforming K-12 Education and is a leader who knows the value of "learning without limits."

> **RONNIE PRICE**, *vice president of People, Culture and Equity, College of Southern Maryland*

Donnie Earl is progressive… young… hip…

> **MARA SHALHOUP**, *writer, "The Young Shepherd," in Creative Loafing*

[Dr. Burks] is insightful and painfully honest about what it takes to get [organizations] and professionals to perform at high levels as well as the tremendous amount of sacrifice involved.

> **STANTON E. LAWRENCE, SR., ED.D.**, *assistant superintendent for administration, San Antonio Independent School District*

ALSO BY THE AUTHORS

D.E. PAULK

I Don't Know…The Way Of Knowing

The Holy Bible of Inclusion

*Fully Awake 365: Challenge Your Mind,
Channel Your Power, and Change Your Life*

Available for purchase at mytruthsanctuary.com/products

TONY LAMAIR BURKS II

Bought Wisdom: Tales of Living and Learning

*Leave with Love: A Spiritual Guide to Succession Planning
and Transitions for Charismatic Church Founders*
by Bishop Dr. Barbara Lewis King
(with Tony Lamair Burks II)

*The Journey to Authenticity: 8 Secrets
to Getting the Life You Desire*
by Mitchell L. Jones (with Tony Lamair Burks II)

Queen Sugar Learning Companion
www.queensugar101.org

SHI(F)T HAPPENS,
DON'T LOSE YOUR SHI(R)T

Architecting Inclusion While
Maintaining Financial Solvency

BISHOP D.E. PAULK
Rev. Dr. Tony Lamair Burks II

Layout and Design by Tony Lamair Burks II

Copyediting by Jonathan T. Simmons, Braxton L. Nelson, and Tony Lamair Burks II

Cover Design by Chris Haler, Square One Creative Group

This workbook is a learning component of INCLUSION 2024 Shi(F)t Happens, Don't Lose Your Shi(R)t hosted by the International Communion of Expanding Consciousness (I.C.E.C.) and Spirit and Truth Sanctuary.

Printed and published in the United States of America

Shi(F)t Happens, Don't Lose Your Shi(R)t: *Architecting Inclusion While Maintaining Financial Solvency* / D.E. Paulk and Tony Lamair Burks II— *1st ed.*
ISBN 978-1-7370451-8-2

PRAYER OF SURRENDER

Spirit of Truth,
CARRY ME where You will,
BRING TO ME what You will,
TAKE FROM ME what You will,
AWAKEN IN ME what You will.
The Christ HUMAN is AROUND me.
The Christ MIND is IN me.
The Christ POWER flows THROUGH me.
And, the Christ MYSTERY exists AS me.
I believe it.
I perceive it.
And, now I receive it!
I am surrendered.
Amen.

DEDICATION

This workbook is dedicated to the memory of my mentor, Bishop Carlton D'Metrius Pearson, a man we lovingly called *CDP*. His unwavering faith, visionary leadership, and boundless love have left an indelible mark on my life and the lives of countless others. His courage to preach the message of inclusion and his tireless efforts to bring people together regardless of race, denomination, or background continue to inspire and guide us.

It is also dedicated to the many beautiful spirits, brave souls, and brilliant sojourners who are sufficiently courageous to further his life's work of love and legacy of inclusion. Your commitment to creating inclusive spiritual communities is a testament to CDP's enduring influence and a beacon of hope for the future.

To the ministers and laypeople globally who are haunted by visions of transitioning their spiritual communities into inclusion; yet, harassed with concerns of maintaining financial solvency, this work is for you. May you find strength, inspiration, and practical wisdom within these pages to navigate the challenges you face and to realize the transformative potential of an inclusive faith.

CONTENTS

ACKNOWLEDGMENTS

From Bishop Paulk:

To my wife, the love of my life, mother of my children, greatest supporter, boldest defender, tireless co-pastor, and fearless co-creator on this courageous adventure…"my Brandin" Paulk. I see you! And, to my amazing children, Esther and Micah. Thank you to "Us Four" for taking the risk with me and for choosing the road less traveled!

To my parents, Pastors Don and Clariece Paulk. Thank you for your open hearts and minds, courageous involvement in Civil and Human Rights, and for standing by me at all times and in all ways.

To my sister, LaDonna Paulk Diaz. Thank you for being a steady hand, calming spirit, loving voice, and a peaceful, sane presence of reason and balance in my life, for all of my life.

To Randy Renfroe, my lifelong best friend, and to Benny Grizzell and the Spirit & Truth Sanctuary staff, pastors, volunteers and members who are the proof that transitioning into Inclusion can work. Without your courage and faithfulness, this work would merely be a blissful hypothetical. Your boldness and brilliance are the demonstration of this communication.

To Rev. Jon Scott (co-founder of the I.C.E.C.), and to Pastor Mike Williams, for stating the case, staying the course, and for being true brothers and fellow architects in this amazing work of inclusion. CDP is so proud of you…of us!

To CDP's family, Gina Gauthier, Julian Pearson, and Majeste Pearson, for sharing your husband and father with the world. I know his mission came at a high cost.

To all of CDP's spiritual children and followers all over the world.

Thank you for your courageous curiosity and for believing in the possibility of a more loving way to worship and live.

Finally, to Dr. Tony Lamair Burks II. Thank you for seeing this vision in its infancy and for the countless hours of sweat equity and priceless brilliance you have invested in this project!

From Dr. Burks:

Books—of any genre, of any length—owe their existence to a cadre of encouragers and supporters: seen and unseen, sung and unsung.

Thank you to Bishop D. E. Paulk and Pastor Brandi Paulk for entrusting me to "co-architect" this workbook in support of furthering the Inclusion Journeys of seekers of truth.

Thank you to my immediate family—Thandiwe DeShazor, Jurney DeShazor-Burks, and J. Ceasar Hingleton—for granting me grace and for putting up with my absence as I focused on completing this workbook. And to my parents—Janice Potter Burks and the everliving Tony Lamair Burks—thank you for the gift of life and for being my greatest cheerleaders.

Thank you to my best friends— Anthony Bostic, Piaget Todd Averyhart, Jesse White, and Dr. Rodney Boone—my fraternity brothers—Marcus Fields, Christopher Jolley, Dr. Harley Etienne, Julian Cobb, Pierre Edwards, and Jordan Collins—and my Aces—Yakima Rhinehart, Valerie Bouldin, Angel McCurdy, Chantel Mullen, and Kelly Nance—for being guideposts and wise counsel.

Thank you to my executive assistant, Jonathan T. Simmons, and my friend, Braxton L. Nelson, for editing and conducting independent reviews of the workbook.

WHY *THIS* WORKBOOK?

This workbook is a vital resource for spiritual leaders, ministers, and laity committed to fostering inclusive communities of faith—and I am thrilled to share it with you.

Inspired by the profound teachings and legacy of my mentor, Bishop Carlton D'Metrius Pearson, we've put together practical guidance, inspirational wisdom, and actionable strategies to help you navigate the journey towards inclusion.

I believe this workbook is crucial because it empowers leaders like you to create environments where everyone, no matter their race, denomination, or background, feels valued and embraced. By promoting a message of universal love and acceptance, we're not just honoring CDP's groundbreaking vision—we're also paving the way for a more harmonious and inclusive future for all our faith communities.

Join us in this journey, and let's build a more inclusive world together!

OUR GLOSSARY OF SELECT TERMS

Why on earth would we put a glossary at the beginning of this workbook? In a nutshell, our desire is for you to be in the know from the get-go! We want you to dive into this workbook with confidence, without tripping over any jargon or scratching your head about new terms.

Think of our glossary as your VIP pass to understanding all the key concepts and buzzwords we'll be using in this workbook and throughout *Inclusion 2024*, a conference hosted by I.C.E.C. If you get a chance to read the definitions of these terms before your first session, we promise they'll help you have a smooth, enlightening, and enjoyable journey through the world of inclusion. Let's take a quick tour of these terms:

- *Architecting Inclusion*: Intentionally approaching the communication and facilitation of inclusion in a way that is both palpable and palatable for those curious about inclusion and seeking a bigger and better vision and version of the Ultimate Reality we call "God."

  Define this term in your own words: _____

- *Apokatastasis*: The original Christian doctrine espoused by many of the early church fathers; the belief held that every person has been, or will be, reconciled to God, and everything in creation will eventually return to a perfect state.

  Define this term in your own words: _____

- *Azusa*: Refers to a series of religious meetings in Los Angeles, California, in 1906 known for starting the modern Pentecostal movement. It also refers to the Azusa Conferences founded by Bishop Carlton Pearson that gave preachers and gospel musicians a platform to showcase their talents and introduce them to a wider audience of people.

Define this term in
your own words: ————————————————————
————————————————————

- *Bibliolatry*: The worship, idolization, and excessive reverence of the Bible; holding the written Bible as both literal and God's infallible Word to mankind.

Define this term in
your own words: ————————————————————
————————————————————

- *Christ Mind/Christ Presence*: The eternal presence of love and wisdom found in Jesus; yet, not limited to a specific person.

Define this term in
your own words: ————————————————————
————————————————————

- *Cosmology*: The study or belief of the origin and organization of the universe.

Define this term in
your own words: ————————————————————
————————————————————

- *Dogmatic*: Sticking strictly to a set of beliefs (dogmas) without questioning them.

Define this term in
your own words: ————————————————————
————————————————————

- *Ecumenical*: Efforts to unite the universal Christian family as well as diverse spiritual communities and disparate faith traditions.

Define this term in
your own words: ————————————————————
————————————————————

- *Eucharist*: A symbolic Christian ceremony where bread and wine are shared to remember the last meal of Jesus the Christ.

Define this term in
your own words: ————————————————————
————————————————————

- *Evangelical*: Christians who prescribe to Jesus being the only way to salvation / God, and who focus on spreading their faith by conversion.

**Define this term in
your own words:**

- *Exegesis*: The careful explanation and interpretation of a religious text to understand its true meaning; specifically critical study of the Bible (including the etymology of original languages).

  **Define this term in
  your own words:**

- *Finished Work*: A belief that the death of Jesus the Christ and his resurrection completed all the work needed for the salvation of humanity.

  **Define this term in
  your own words:**

- *Ganesh Puja*: A Hindu worship ritual paying homage to Lord Ganesh ("remover of obstacles"); Ganesh is pictured as an elephant headed deity.

  **Define this term in
  your own words:**

- *Gospel of Inclusion*: Simply the Good News of the Gospel; according to Bishop Carlton Pearson, "everything evolves out of One, into One and ultimately as One. God is God and…would not have excluded anybody."

  **Define this term in
  your own words:**

- *Hermeneutics*: The study of how to interpret and understand religious texts.

  **Define this term in
  your own words:**

- *Higher Dimensions*: A ministry founded by Bishop Carlton Pearson in Tulsa, Oklahoma, and one of the first Black megachurches in the United States of America.

Define this term in
your own words:

- *Krishna*: A major Hindu god, known for his playful and loving nature, who has striking parallels and connections with Jesus the Christ predating Christianity by three thousand years.

Define this term in
your own words:

- *Liturgical*: The formal, public worship and rituals in a church.

Define this term in
your own words:

- *Metaphysical*: An exploration of deeper meanings beyond the physical world; often referred to in spiritual teachings connecting the mind with the body and the outer expression.

Define this term in
your own words:

- *Mithras (also Mithra)*: An ancient god worshiped in the Roman Empire, often linked to the sun and light. The worship of this ancient god—who was born on December 25—includes a sacrament of "the bread and the wine" predating Christianity by just over a thousand years.

Define this term in
your own words:

- *New Thought Christianity*: A spiritual movement emphasizing the power of the mind, the divinity of humans, and the idea that God is present in everything.

Define this term in
your own words:

- *Savior Characters*: Important divine figures in different religions who save or help people.

Define this term in
your own words: ....
....

- *Soteriology*: The study of religious beliefs about salvation, how people are saved, and what it means to be saved.

Define this term in
your own words: ....
....

- *Text Neutrality*: A mindset allowing us to appreciate eternal wisdom in all its forms.

Define this term in
your own words: ....
....

- *Transcendence*: The experience of going beyond normal physical or spiritual limits.

Define this term in
your own words: ....
....

- *Transcendent Worship*: Worship that helps people feel they are connecting with something beyond the ordinary world.

Define this term in
your own words: ....
....

- *Univocality:* The attempt to force the Bible to speak in one voice (that is, the Voice of God) despite human errors, the passage of time, and contradictions.

Define this term in
your own words: ....
....

- *Weltanschauung*: A person's overall worldview or perspective on life and the universe.

Define this term in
your own words: ....
....

YOUR GLOSSARY OF TERMS

As you walk along this Inclusion Journey, you'll likely encounter new terms and phrases that you'd like to remember. We invite you to use this space to jot down these words and phrases (and if drawing or doodling will help, please do so!).

_____

_____

_____

_____

_____

_____

_____

_____

_____

_____

_____

_____

_____

_____

_____

_____

_____

_____

_____

_____

_____

_____

_____

INTRODUCTION
My "CDP"

I am a spiritual son of Bishop Carlton D. Pearson. His children, Julian and Majeste, refer to me as their father's successor. Bishop Pearson called me his "First Son of Inclusion." I have known CDP since 1978–I was 5 years old. He spoke at our church every year, most years multiple times, refusing to stay in a hotel but rather in our home, with us, his extended family. There is no quantifiable way to calculate the countless hours CDP and I spent sitting around casually talking, uncontrollably laughing, occasionally crying, passionately dreaming, unpredictably pontificating, and randomly ranting about everything from religious constructs and political ideologies to church mothers' hats, deacons' flopping dentures, choir members' crooked wigs, and church folks' generally wearisome ways.

My predecessor, Archbishop Earl P. Paulk, Jr. (Civil Rights pioneer and church reformer in his own right), consecrated CDP into the bishopric in 1996. Thirteen years later, CDP and I eulogized my predecessor together on the stage of the world's first Neo-gothic Pentecostal cathedral built by my family. At that time, I found myself managing an epic storm CDP bravely helped me navigate. I loved him for that! And, I am forever indebted to him for his loyalty to my family during a very difficult moment. I would like to boast that CDP was partial to my family in this way. Yet, the evidence of his life would disprove my assertion as he walked with hundreds of ministers through their valleys of death and shameful, shaky, shadowy seasons.

As a child, CDP dreamed of traveling the world, preaching on every continent, and bringing God's people together regardless of race or denomination. And, he accomplished it all at a very young age. His church, *Higher Dimensions* in Tulsa, Oklahoma, became a megachurch and internationally known ministry, solidifying his status as a bonafide Gospel icon. He advised presidents and counseled professional athletes. Coming from very humble beginnings, he satisfied commonly held definitions of church success while realizing and redefining ministerial prowess in the Evangelical world.

Under CDP's leadership, the Azusa Conferences filled arenas all over America and launched the musical ministries and preaching careers of many of the modern-day Christian ministers who have become household names. He seemed to possess the vision of a gospel talent scout, embodying this mystical sense of knowing and divine discernment that recognized anointing, charisma, and potential in relatively unknown ministers and musicians. He even admitted to me he had turned down six-figure bribes on several occasions from ambitious preachers eager for their shot at the Azusa stage, which became known as a gospel tarmac providing runway for flights into preaching fame.

But, in a turn of events, a date with fate was about to announce its presence. At the height of this mania, CDP was about to discover and then platform a guest, not merely to the Pentecostal-Charismatic stage, but to the world stage. This artist was not destined to facilitate a good shout. This preacher would not be asked to foster an emotional breakthrough or even a genuinely transcendent worship experience. CDP's very last Azusa guest would shake the very foundations of the cosmology and culture of Christendom.

While sitting atop the apex of "Gospel Hollywood's" pinnacle, his specific purpose became crystal clear. The *Higher Dimensions* success, Azusa fame, and international influence were all part of a plan, a divine setup, designed to shed light on an ancient mystery privileged only to the higher mind, confined to the halls of academia, and held in abeyance by scholars.

CDP's mission was to bring an old doctrine, and an original idea, back to the surface. An idea that had remained hidden from most Christians for over 1,500 years. What was this idea? *INCLUSION*! And, it has many names. In Evangelical spaces, it can appear as "The Finished Work," "Ultimate Reconciliation," or "The Restoration of All Things." A bit more unapologetically, it exists in the Anglican genre as "Christian Universalism" or "Universal Salvation." From the theological narrative of Early Church Fathers, we find it as *apokatastasis* or creation returning to a condition of perfection. This concept, once shrouded in obscurity, was brought to the forefront by CDP's bold vision and unwavering commitment to a message of universal altruism and love.

CDP's journey was not without its challenges. As he began to preach the Gospel of Inclusion, he faced intense scrutiny and criticism from the Evangelical community. Many labeled him a heretic, and his once-thriving ministry faced significant backlash. Yet, CDP remained steadfast, believing deeply in the transformative power of his message. He knew the path he was forging was not just for his time, but for future generations that would continue to build on the trail he blazed.

I remember vividly the day CDP shared with me his vision for a more inclusive faith. We were sitting in my living room, the afternoon sun casting long shadows across the floor. He spoke with passion, his eyes alight with the conviction of his beliefs. "Inclusion is not just a doctrine," he said, "It's a way of life. It's about seeing the Divine in everyone and everything, and recognizing that we are all part of a greater whole."

As I listened, I felt a profound sense of clarity. CDP's words resonated deeply with me, and I realized his vision was not just his own, but a universal truth with the power to transform lives and communities. From that moment on, I committed myself to carrying forward his legacy, to preaching the message of inclusion and to building a spiritual community that embodies these principles.

CDP's influence on my life and ministry is immeasurable. He taught me to dream big, to take risks, and to stand firm in my convictions. His unwavering support and mentorship have been a guiding light, helping me navigate the challenges and triumphs of my own journey. As I reflect on his life and legacy, I am filled with gratitude for the many ways he has shaped and inspired me.

Inclusion is a journey, not a destination. It requires us to constantly expand our understanding, to embrace new perspectives, and to open our hearts to the diverse expressions of the divine. As we move forward, let us honor CDP's legacy by continuing to preach and live the message of inclusion, by creating welcoming and affirming communities, and by seeing the Divine in all people.

May this workbook serve you as a faithful guide along your Inclusion Journey. Now, are you ready to talk some Shi(f)t?

Bishop D.E. Paulk
Decatur, Georgia
September 2024

SURVIVING THE SHIFT
The 12 Principles of Inclusion

The number 12 holds significant symbolic meaning across various world religions. In Christianity, it is prominently featured with the 12 apostles of Jesus Christ, representing the foundation of the church. In Islam, 12 Imams are revered in Shia tradition, believed to be spiritual and temporal leaders. Hinduism and Buddhism also emphasize the number 12 through the 12 Adityas, deities representing the sun, and the 12 Nidanas, the chain of causation that leads to the cycle of existence, respectively. In Judaism, 12 signifies completeness, seen in the 12 stones on the High Priest's breastplate, each stone representing a tribe of Israel. To this end, there are *12 Principles of Inclusion*:

- *Intellectual Curiosity*: Maintaining an interest in learning, unlearning, and relearning through books and resources—including people—to deepen an understanding of inclusive practices.
- *Respect for Diversity*: Knowing, valuing, and understanding differences in race, gender, sexuality, culture, and beliefs among individuals.
- *Universal Acceptance*: Embracing all individuals regardless of backgrounds, and ensuring everyone feels welcomed and valued.
- *Non-judgmental Stance*: Creating a safe space where everyone can express themselves without fear of judgment or exclusion.
- *Open Dialogue*: Encouraging open and honest discussions to understand divergent perspectives.
- *Empathy and Compassion*: Understanding the feelings of others and acting with kindness and consideration.
- *Common Ground*: Finding and emphasizing shared beliefs and values to foster unity.
- *Allies and Support*: Building connections and ties with diverse individuals and groups build and nurture inclusive environments.

- *Patient Progress*: Allowing time for individuals and communities to adapt and evolve towards inclusion without forcing rapid change.
- *Adaptability*: Embracing an openness and flexibility with practices, language, and rituals to ensure the engagement and involvement of diverse groups.
- *Celebrating All Wins*: Acknowledging all progress—big or small—along the Inclusion Journey.
- *Holistic Approach*: Considering the emotional, spiritual, intellectual, and practical elements to create a comprehensive and sustainable inclusive culture.

I believe these 12 principles are interwoven in the 25 *Inclusion Journey Insights* I offer. Together they will help you and your members navigate new semantics and unfamiliar terms; as well as diverse sacred texts and worship experiences. Much of this is based on over two decades of experience in transitioning an Evangelical church into an inclusive ministry we describe as, "The Trendiest, Friendliest, Happiest, Most Radically Inclusive Worship Experience in Atlanta."

OUR PRAYER
Eternal Mystery,
thank You for freeing me
from the bondage of my past.
Strengthen me to walk into freedom.
Awaken me to the power
I have to change my perception.
Help me choose the highest thoughts
available to me. Amen.

— D.E. Paulk and LaDonna Paulk Diaz
from *Fully Awake 365* (2022)

THINK OUTSIDE THE INCLUSION BOX:
DON'T USE THE WORD

Only babies in wet diapers welcome change. This adage humorously captures the natural and common resistance many people have about change. This aversion to change is stronger within established institutions like the church. As a minister or a layperson, you are positioned as a change agent. This work of navigating resistance requires wisdom, patience, and strategic thinking.

Change within a church often involves managing three critical phases: *Endings*, *The Wilderness*, and *New Beginnings* (Bridges, 2016). Each phase requires clear communication. It is critical for you to clearly communicate the *purpose*, paint a vivid *picture* of the future, develop and articulate a detailed *plan*, and share defined roles or *positions* for everyone involved.

Phase One - Endings: Change begins with acknowledging key practices, beliefs, or traditions may need to end. This phase can be the most challenging, as it involves letting go of familiar and comfortable ways:

> ***Purpose***: Ask, "Why are we doing this?" As a minister or a layperson, communicate the need for change by framing it within the context of God's greater purpose. I invite you to emphasize the goal is to better align your faith community with the principles of God's unconditional and radical love. For example, you might say, "We are embarking on this journey to reflect God's love more fully in our community, ensuring everyone feels valued and included."

Picture: Ask, "What will things look like?" As a minister or a layperson, paint a vivid picture of what your faith community will look like once you have embraced the principles of God's unconditional and radical love. I encourage you to use storytelling and examples from other communities that have successfully navigated similar changes. For example, you might say, "Imagine a church where everyone, regardless of background, feels welcomed and loved—a place where God's love is evident in every interaction."

Plan: Ask, "How will we make this change?" As a minister or a layperson, outline an actionable plan for transitioning from the old ways to the new. I invite you to break down the process into manageable steps to avoid overwhelming your faith community. For example, you might say, "We will begin by hosting small group discussions to gather input and hear concerns. Next, we'll introduce new outreach programs that embody radical love."

Position: Ask, "What role must I play in this change?" As a minister or a layperson, identify people and assign specific roles to them. I encourage you to make it clear everyone has a part to play in this Inclusion Journey. For example, you might say, "We need volunteers to lead the discussion groups, team members for the outreach programs, and prayer warriors to support this transition with their intercession."

Phase Two - The Wilderness: This period is a time of uncertainty and exploration. Your faith community navigates the unknown and adapts to new ways of thinking and doing during this phase:

Purpose: Ask, "Why are we doing this?" As a minister or a layperson, reinforce the purpose regularly as a way of keeping your faith community focused and motivated. I invite you to remind them this Inclusion Journey is about embodying God's love more authentically. For example, you might say, "As we navigate this Wilderness, remember our ultimate goal is to become a more inclusive reflection of Christ's love."

Picture: Ask, "What will things look like?" As a minister or a layperson, continue to share stories and examples of what the future holds. I encourage you to use testimonies from those who are already experiencing the benefits of the change. For example, you might say, "Look at how our new outreach programs are already bringing people together. This is just the beginning of the beautiful transformation we're working towards."

Plan: Ask, "How will we make this change?" As a minister or a layperson, adapt and refine the plan as needed based on feedback and experiences. I invite you to ensure your faith community knows the steps are flexible and can be adjusted to meet the community's needs. For example, you might say, "Based on your feedback, we're adjusting our approach to make our discussion groups more inclusive and accessible to everyone."

Position: Ask, "What role must I play in this change?" As a minister or a layperson, keep people engaged by highlighting their roles and contributions. I encourage you to celebrate small wins and acknowledge the efforts of individuals and groups. For example, you might say, "Thank you to our discussion leaders for their dedication. Your work is paving the way for our inclusion transformation."

Phase Three - New Beginnings: In this phase, changes take root and become the new norm. This phase is about solidifying the new practices and ensuring they are sustainable:

Purpose: Ask, "Why are we doing this?" As a minister or a layperson, reiterate the purpose over and over. I encourage you to reinforce the significance of the journey and the positive outcomes achieved. For example, you might say, "We've come this far because we believed in reflecting God's radical love. Our new beginning is a testament to our commitment to this divine purpose."

Picture: Ask, "What will things look like?" As a minister or a layperson, celebrate the new reality and showcase the positive changes. I invite you to use visual and anecdotal evidence to highlight the transformation. For example, you might say, "Look around and see the diversity in our congregation, the new faces, and the renewed sense of community. This is what God's love looks like in action."

Plan: Ask, "How will we make this change?" As a minister or a layperson, establish ongoing plans to maintain and build upon the changes. I encourage you to ensure there are systems in place to support continuous improvement and inclusion. For example, you might say, "We will continue to have regular training and development sessions to keep our focus on inclusion. Our new committees will ensure our practices remain aligned with our mission."

Position: Ask, "What role must I play in this change?" As a minister or a layperson, define ongoing roles and responsibilities to maintain the new practices. I invite you to encourage everyone to take ownership of the change and be proactive in its sustainability. For example, you might say, "Everyone here plays a vital role in maintaining this inclusive environment. Whether you're a greeter, a prayer leader, or part of our outreach team, your commitment is essential to our continued success."

I think it's important for you to think outside the box to understand the cultural landscape of your faith community. Understanding the diversity within and beyond your faith community is crucial. Terms like "inclusion" or "universal salvation" can trigger fear or caution…even confusion. Instead, consider using phrases like "the restoration of all things" or "in the sovereignty of God, no one will be lost."

While inclusion is an important aspect, introducing it too early can create resistance. Instead, we can use the strategy of camouflaging inclusion under terms which resonate more broadly with the congregation. In the Book of Esther, the word "God" is never mentioned, yet God's influence and guidance are unmistakable. Esther, a Hebrew in camouflage, navigates a foreign court and saves her people without openly revealing her identity (See *Holy Bible of Inclusion*, p. 279). We can adopt a similar approach by framing our message of inclusion using familiar words, experiences, and stories. I have learned that four common concepts can derail Inclusion Journeys within faith communities:

The Rapture: Some in the Latinx religious community may accept the Finished Work of Calvary (that is, Ultimate Reconciliation) more readily than tampering with beliefs about the second coming or the rapture. Awareness of specific religious and cultural triggers gives those in tricky transition a chance to breathe and reconsider.

Same-Sex Relationships and Homosexuality: Homophobia persists in areas with anti-gay legislation. To architect inclusive spaces globally and across diverse cultures, we must move thoughtfully and strategically. Avoid non-starters and begin with the end in mind. As a straight ally for over 20 years, I've learned achieving critical mass in inclusion requires avoiding actions that might alienate potential supporters. This is in no way an attempt to put anyone back "in the closet" or lessen the freedom of expression and the pursuit of the authentic self.

Hell: Not long after my mentor, Bishop Carlton Pearson, shared the Gospel of Inclusion (2006), he encountered a conundrum,

"What on Earth must we do about Hell?" He wrestled with hell and how it was used by "the saved" and "the sinner" alike to coerce and even threaten God's people into submission. In communities with a painful history of oppression and marginalization, the idea of all people going to the same heaven, regardless of behavior, can be problematic. For example, in the African American Church, the idea of eliminating an eternal hell can be seen as forgiving historical oppressors. However, a deeper understanding of our Divine Parent's nature and a better contextual grasp reveal "fire" in Greek (pur) means to purify, and "brimstone" (theion) refers to God, can help convey the notion of a purifying, medicinal process. In this application, God is purging creation rather than the "all or nothing" approach polarizing God as either wiping the slate clean or eternally torturing transgressors (See *The Holy Bible of Inclusion* pp. 144-169).

Jesus the Christ and Other Divine Figures: Inclusion often leads to a broader Christ-consciousness which transcends (yet includes) the historical Jesus. For those deeply attached to Jesus, introducing other savior figures or suggesting Jesus is not the only path to God can end the conversation prematurely (See *The Holy Bible of Inclusion* pp. 233-272). Rather than hosting an interfaith day or initially singing a Hindu mantra, begin this transition with an occasional light seasoning of diverse divine figures who taught similar ideas as Jesus. This will help ease people into rethinking the bigness of God.

So now what? In *Journey to Authenticity: The Eight Secrets to Getting the Life You Desire* (2016), Dr. Tony Lamair Burks II defines *LifeWork as* "Homework for living an authentic life" involving states of being and doing, which lead to having all one desires. *LifeWork* and this workbook—taken together—are the foundation of our never-ending Inclusion Journey. Below is your first *LifeWork* assignment; you'll find *LifeWork* at the end of each *Inclusion Journey Insight* chapter.

YOUR *LifeWork*

Message: As a minister or a layperson, emphasize the profound importance of embodying both unconditional and radical love. God's love is not just all-encompassing and unconditional, but also radical in its inclusion, challenging us to move beyond our comfort zones. This dual concept of love serves as a bridge to broader inclusion and deeper spiritual growth within your community.

Implementation:

- *Teach Through Stories and Sermons*: Utilize stories from various sacred texts to illustrate both unconditional and radical love. Highlight examples of love crossing societal boundaries and personal prejudices.
  - *Facilitate Community Service Projects*: Organize community service projects targeting marginalized groups, encouraging participants to practice radical love by engaging with those outside their usual circles.
  - *Encourage Personal Acts of Love*: Challenge each member to identify and take a specific action reflecting radical love in their personal life, such as reaching out to someone they have previously avoided.
  - *Offer Meditative Practices*: Incorporate meditations focusing on expanding the capacity to love unconditionally and radically, helping the congregation internalize these principles.

Reflection Exercise: As a minister or a layperson, ask yourself these questions: *When have I experienced God's unconditional love in an unexpected way? How did that experience affect me? Where in my life am I still holding back from practicing radical love? What fears or prejudices are limiting me? What steps can I take this week to extend love beyond my usual boundaries? How does my current understanding of God's love challenge me to grow spiritually and emotionally? How can I create opportunities within my community to practice and experience both unconditional and radical love? In what ways can I support others in my congregation to embrace and act upon these principles of love? How can I be more intentional in welcoming those who are different from me into my community and personal life?* Then consider when it makes sense to ask members these same questions.

THINK SPACE: The choice is yours! Take notes, draw, doodle, and brainstorm here to make sense of this particular *Inclusion Insight*.

Affirmation: "I will be the pioneer of a different ending."

— D.E. Paulk and LaDonna Paulk Diaz
from *Fully Awake 365* (2022)

Inclusion Insight 2

COMMON SENSE KICKOFF:
ASK THE BIG QUESTIONS

Is God's earth project a failure?
Is God a teacher or a torturer?
Is God's purpose purgative, seeking to cleanse and renew?
Or is it punitive, driven by retribution and vengeance?

These are not just questions; but profound contemplations piercing through the surface of our faith, challenging us to dive deeper into the very essence of the Divine. When we begin with the nature and character of God, we aren't merely opening a door; we are laying out a vast foundation. This foundation is broad enough to support the weight of countless perspectives, and wide enough to embrace the diversity of human thought. This foundation—like the earth itself—can house an infinite variety of ideas, each one a room in the sprawling mansion of God's understanding (See *The Holy Bible of Inclusion* pp. 144-145).

In our Father's "house" are indeed many mansions—a phrase rich with metaphor and meaning. Within the boundless Mind of the Universe, there are countless expressions, each an unique facet of the Divine consciousness. Just as a mansion has rooms for every purpose, from the humble to the grand, so too does God's house make space for all levels of spiritual awareness. The literal mind, perhaps still at the doorstep of divine wisdom, is nevertheless welcomed within. Even if this mind resides in the mansion's most basic room, it is still part of the household. It is still embraced by the infinite expanses of God's love and patience.

However, when we approach these mysteries through the narrow corridors of chapter, verse, and theological argumentation, we risk closing doors rather than opening them. These discussions can quickly become walls dividing us, leading us down paths of separation and exclusion. Instead, our starting point should be questions that illuminate, questions that cast God's character in a light so expansive and glorious it becomes nearly impossible to diminish or dismiss (See *The Holy Bible of Inclusion* pp. 56-59).

Consider, for instance, the comparison between Adam's act, which brought death into the world, and Christ's redemptive work, which brought life (The Holy Bible, New King James Version, I Corinthians 15:22). Is it not evident that the power of life and redemption far outweighs the sting of death? This simple yet profound question shifts the focus from the weight of sin to the overwhelming triumph of grace. Another common sense question providing us with yet another angle to open the portal of consciousness is this: will God reclaim all the kingdoms of the world (The Holy Bible, New King James Version, Revelation 11:15), and neglect to reclaim the people in these kingdoms (who are made in the image and likeness of God)? Is God more concerned with lost systems than lost souls? Preoccupied with influence but not with individuals? To picture a desperate, narcissistic God motivated by amassing power, receiving glory and dominating while seemingly nonchalant with the eternal state of humanity is not only grotesque but missing the point completely.

Good theology is more than correct doctrine; it is a way of thinking that leads us to three essential outcomes: glorifying God, fostering peace on earth, and cultivating goodwill among humanity (See *The Holy Bible of Inclusion* pp. 23-24). When we explore God's nature in ways that elevate rather than diminish, we are participating in the divine project of healing and reconciling the world. We bring glory to God not just through words, but through an active life reflecting God's love, justice, and mercy. With this, peace on earth becomes not just a hope, but a tangible reality, as our understanding of God's inclusive and redemptive nature compels us to be peacemakers. And goodwill among humanity flourishes when we see each person, each belief, as another room in the mansion of God's house—a place where all are welcome, and all are cherished.

YOUR *LifeWork*

Message: As a minister or a layperson, remember God's nature is both loving and inclusive, constantly inviting us to understand and embrace the diversity within God's creation. This understanding can lead to deeper faith, stronger unity among members, and a more welcoming spiritual community.

Implementation:
- *Host Discussion Groups*: Organize weekly discussion groups where members of your faith community can openly share their thoughts on God's nature. Focus on how God's love and inclusivity shape their personal faith and relationships within the community. Consider developing a sermon series or study group about "The Nature of God: Redemption, Love, and Inclusivity."
- *Serve the Community*: Engage in or organize volunteer efforts serving historically marginalized or underrepresented communities. This will allow your community to live out God's inclusive love in practical ways.
- *Create Artistic Representations*: Encourage members to create visual or artistic representations of *God's House of Many Mansions*, reflecting the diversity and inclusion within God's nature. Display these works in your place of worship as a reminder of God's ever-expanding love.

Reflection Exercise: As a minister or a layperson, ask yourself these questions: *How has my understanding of God's loving and inclusive nature evolved over time? In what ways do I see God's love reflected in the diversity within my faith community? How do my beliefs about God's nature influence my interactions with others, particularly those from different backgrounds or beliefs? In what ways can I use my personal or collective experiences to inspire ongoing efforts to embrace and celebrate diversity within my community?* Then consider when it makes sense to ask members these same questions.

Affirmation: "I affirm that I am not my race, gender, sexual orientation, religion, political party or country of origin. I declare my freedom from form."

— D.E. Paulk and LaDonna Paulk Diaz
from *Fully Awake 365* (2022)

KEEPING IT 100:
INCLUSION ≠ LICENSE TO MISBEHAVE

As I reflect on the essence of this journey, it is important to acknowledge a profound truth: *inclusion is not an excuse for recklessness.* Yes, we are reminded in Romans 8:38-39 (The Holy Bible, New King James Version) nothing can separate us from the love of God, and John 1:29 (The Holy Bible, New King James Version) tells us the Lamb of God takes away the sin of the world. Given all of this, we might then ask, "So what is sin?" If sin, (*hamartia* in Greek - "offense") has been taken away, do we still sin? Yes, we "miss the mark" (in Greek *hamartano*). But, whose mark are we missing? Is it set by Moses, Paul, or someone else? If ticking off God is no longer the issue, then who or what do we sin against? The answer is clear: *ourselves*. In truth, when we sin or miss the mark, we go against our own divinity. We do this if we live in ways that disrupt our peace and wellbeing. This understanding doesn't diminish Christ's work; rather, it calls us to be vigilant in our daily lives. Even if there is no future hell, we must be careful not to create one here and now.

Inclusion isn't about embracing anything and everything; it's about welcoming "whosoever will" while fostering environments of peace and joy. Inclusion needs people who are stable, responsible, and committed to making good choices. It's not just for those who have lost everything and are seeking a fresh start—it's also for those who have learned to navigate their divine creativity responsibly. We must constantly ask ourselves, "Is it working for *me*?"—a question guiding our personal peace and joy. And we must also ask, "Is it working for *us*?" As architects of inclusion, our personal freedoms must align with the collective good, ensuring our spiritual practices lead to growth and maturity for everyone involved.

YOUR *LifeWork*

Message: As a minister or a layperson, explore the essential balance between personal freedom and communal responsibility. True inclusion requires more than just welcoming all; it involves a commitment to actions fostering both individual well-being and collective harmony. While grace provides the foundation for inclusion, it does not excuse harmful behavior toward ourselves or others. We must continuously align our actions with the greater good, recognizing personal happiness should never come at the expense of communal well-being. Use the metaphor of "missing the mark" to illustrate the importance of this alignment in nurturing a truly inclusive community.

Implementation:
- *Unpack Communal Responsibility*: Invite participants to share stories about times they've "missed the mark" in balancing personal freedom with communal responsibility. Encourage open discussion on how they corrected their course and the role of self-governance in fostering peace and inclusion.
- *Organize a Decision-Making Workshop*: Conduct a workshop using role-playing exercises to explore scenarios where individual desires conflict with the needs of the community. Highlight the importance of decision-making processes benefitting both the individual and the collective.
- *Develop an Accountability Partner System*: Pair participants with accountability partners to support each other in aligning their actions with the collective good. Encourage regular check-ins to discuss challenges and successes in maintaining this balance.
- *Lead a Study on Grace and Responsibility*: Organize a study group to delve deeper into the concept of grace as it relates to responsibility. Use scriptural references and other spiritual teachings emphasizing while grace is inclusive, it calls for actions promoting the wellbeing of all.

Reflection Exercise: As a minister or a layperson, ask yourself these questions: *When have I mistaken inclusion for a free pass to act poorly or negatively without accountability? Where in my life have I prioritized personal happiness over the greater good? How can I better align my actions with peace and well-being for both myself and others? What practices help me balance my personal freedom with the collective good? What steps can I take to become a more responsible member of my inclusive community? How can I encourage others to see the importance of communal responsibility in our shared spiritual journey?* Then consider when it makes sense to ask members these same questions.

THINK SPACE: The choice is yours! Take notes, draw, doodle, and brainstorm here to make sense of this particular *Inclusion Insight*.

Prayer: "Spirit of Inclusion, help me to learn from the sin of Jonah. I have been included. Strengthen me to include. Amen."

— D.E. Paulk and LaDonna Paulk Diaz
from *Fully Awake 365* (2022)

SEMANTICS:
SPEAK THEIR LANGUAGE

As your congregation grows and evolves to embrace greater inclusion, the language you use becomes an essential part of your Inclusion Journey. Terms play a key role in this transformation. Introducing new words, readings, and expressions can often stir discomfort; yet, it also offers an opportunity to connect these fresh ideas with familiar concepts. In a recent devotional, I chose to use 365 different names for God, with the goal of helping our congregation grow comfortable with the variety of expressions speaking to the Divine nature. The intention was to honor the one God who defies any single name.

In a more inclusive setting, we naturally move away from rigid interpretations of scripture, opening ourselves up to a broader understanding of the Divine (See *Fully Awake 365*). However, as we navigate this shift, it's essential to address pressing concerns. Many of these concerns come from unfamiliar language. By drawing clear connections between new and familiar terms—like explaining "Source" as God, "vibration" as attitude, and the "law of attraction" as a close cousin of the scripture, "as a [person] thinks in [their] heart[s], so [are they]" (The Holy Bible, New King James Version, Proverbs 23:7). When we take this approach, we ease the pain some experience on their Inclusion Journey.

Language can either create division or build bridges. By carefully selecting words that resonate with the congregation, we can transform potential conflicts into opportunities for growth (See *The Holy Bible of Inclusion* pp. 279-281). If the Holy Spirit enables us to speak so everyone can understand, then we are surely capable of introducing new language that fosters both inclusion and understanding. (Ammerman et al., p.123).

YOUR *LifeWork*

Message: As a minister or a layperson, consider the profound impact of language on shaping our understanding of faith and spirituality. Reflect on how embracing new spiritual terms, while ensuring they are accessible and relatable, can deepen your relationship with God and foster a more inclusive community. Follow the example of Jesus using parables to convey profound truths, and recognize how the Holy Spirit empowers us to communicate effectively. By thoughtfully introducing and integrating new language, we can bridge the gap between tradition and inclusion, nurturing a church environment where everyone feels understood and valued.

Implementation:

- *Sermon Series and Study Guides*: Develop a sermon series introducing one new spiritual term each week, connecting it to a traditional Christian concept. Provide clear explanations and practical examples to help the congregation embrace these new terms. Create a brief study guide to accompany each sermon, offering members an opportunity for deeper reflection throughout the week on the new term and its spiritual significance.
- *Retreat for Ministers and Laypeople*: Facilitate a retreat aimed at developing communication strategies aligned with the Holy Spirit's guidance. Use this time to brainstorm and role-play scenarios where new language may be introduced to the congregation. Develop a shared approach to ensure consistency and clarity in messaging.
- *Resource Development*: Collaborate with other like-minded faith communities to create resources (e.g., pamphlets, videos, blogs) explaining new spiritual terms and concepts in an accessible way. Distribute these resources within the church community. Provide tools and techniques for ministers and laypeople to incorporate this language into their teaching and community interactions.

- *Feedback Mechanisms*: Establish regular feedback sessions where congregation members can share their thoughts and experiences about the new language being introduced. Use this feedback to refine and improve your communication strategies.

Reflection Exercise: As a minister or a layperson, ask yourself these questions: *How did the introduction of new spiritual terms resonate with my congregation or small group? What strategies did I use to address any resistance or confusion, and were they effective? How has the Holy Spirit influenced my approach to communicating new spiritual concepts? What feelings or thoughts arose as you explored unfamiliar language within your faith practice? How can I support other ministers and laypeople in navigating these linguistic transitions?* Then consider when it makes sense to ask members these same questions.

THINK SPACE: The choice is yours! Take notes, draw, doodle, and brainstorm here to make sense of this particular *Inclusion Insight*.

Prayer: "Spirit of Limitless Expansion, give me courage to live outside of religious systems or finite structures that would hinder my spiritual growth and awakening. My mind is open. I am ready to expand. Amen."

— D.E. Paulk and LaDonna Paulk Diaz
from *Fully Awake 365* (2022)

TEXT TWIST:
INTRODUCING NEW SCRIPTURES

As I have worked to build an interfaith community, I've discovered broadening our spiritual foundation involves bringing diverse sacred texts into our teachings. I am not suggesting you take away the Bible from your members. This is not about diminishing the Bible's significance, but rather about enriching our understanding of it. Instead, on this Inclusion Journey, I offer you another possibility. Our goal is to keep the Bible central, while expanding our view of divine wisdom to include insights from other traditions. This possibility redefines and returns the Bible to them as a sacred text, one more comprehensive and meaningful than before.

When I first quoted Buddha's teaching "All that we are is the result of what we have thought" (Byrom, 1993). I immediately followed with Proverbs 23:7, which declares, "as a man thinks, so is he." (The Holy Bible, New King James Version). This approach reassures our members the Bible remains central, even as we explore other spiritual traditions. Now whenever I reference the *Tao Te Ching*, the *Qur'an*, or other sacred texts, I always return to the Bible, demonstrating the presence of God's truth across humanity without forcing harmonization or assimilation of these texts.

Introducing new religious texts requires a careful balance—a respect for our tradition and an openness to broader spiritual truths. This requires what I call *textual neutrality*, a mindset allowing us to appreciate eternal wisdom in all its forms. God's presence goes beyond the confines of a single book or faith. Achieving this neutrality is complex. It requires us to acknowledge our own interpretive biases, recognizing we all approach new texts through a biblical lens.

Cultivating this perspective is a gradual process. It demands patience, intention, and empathy. Our congregation's higher selves are eager to embrace a more expansive vision of Ultimate Reality, one that is not confined to a single text or faith. Our work as ministers and laypeople involves (co)leading our respective faith communities on this Inclusion Journey, guiding them toward a deeper, more inclusive spiritual awareness.

YOUR *LifeWork*

Message: As a minister or a layperson, embrace the theme of "Bridging the Sacred: Finding Common Ground in All Spiritual Wisdom." Reflect on how the Bible's teachings align with the universal truths found in various spiritual traditions and sacred texts. This exercise invites you to see God's presence beyond the boundaries of any single sacred text, fostering a more inclusive and expansive spiritual understanding.

Implementation:
- *Sermon Preparation*: Prepare a sermon entitled "Seeing God Beyond the Boundaries," where you introduce the concept of textual neutrality. Discuss how it can lead to a broader understanding of God's presence in all sacred texts, not just the Bible.
- *Interfaith Service*: During a service, introduce a quotation from a non-Christian spiritual text (e.g., *Tao Te Ching* or the *Qur'an*) and pair it with a related Bible verse. Emphasize the shared divine principles and discuss how they reflect God's universal wisdom.
- *Comparative Journaling*: Select a spiritual text from a different tradition that you haven't read before. Read it with an open mind, and journal about how the experience impacts your perspective on your own faith.
- *Textual Compilation*: Compile a list of comparative passages from different sacred texts, including the Bible. Use this as a resource for reflection or teaching, helping others see the continuity of divine wisdom across traditions.

- *Community Engagement*: Encourage your congregation or community members to explore spiritual wisdom from other traditions. Provide them with resources or reading lists including texts from various faiths and traditions.

Reflection Exercise: As a minister or a layperson, ask yourself these questions: *How do I feel about integrating teachings from other spiritual texts into my understanding of the Bible? How does comparing these texts with the Bible influence my understanding of God's message? In what ways can recognizing universal truths in other religions deepen my faith in the Bible? What does "textual neutrality" mean to me, and how can I strive to embody it in my spiritual practice? How do I maintain respect for my own faith while remaining open to the wisdom of other traditions? How might recognizing common spiritual truths help me engage more compassionately with those of different faiths?* Then consider when it makes sense to ask members these same questions.

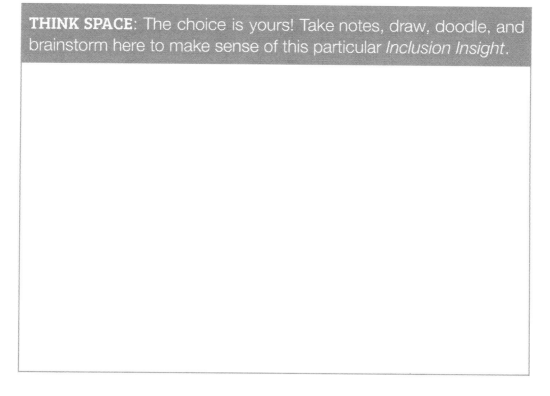

THINK SPACE: The choice is yours! Take notes, draw, doodle, and brainstorm here to make sense of this particular *Inclusion Insight*.

Affirmation: "Sound Doctrine is not tainted by culture, subject to gender, influenced by race, partial to any era of history or area of the world. Sound Doctrine is timeless, universal and exists above humanity's attempt to create God in its own image."

— D.E. Paulk and LaDonna Paulk Diaz
from *Fully Awake 365* (2022)

EXPERIENCE OVER TRADITION: LIVING THE MESSAGE

Experience can be more transformative than tradition. This truth becomes especially clear when exploring the Divine presence beyond the confines of Christianity. While tradition may bind us to the belief God operates exclusively within Christianity, experience reveals a broader truth: God's presence transcends religious boundaries. There's a deep power in experience often surpassing tradition. When we broaden our understanding of where and how God manifests, we open ourselves to new dimensions of faith.

Consider the lives of Gandhi, Thich Nhat Hanh, and the Dalai Lama. Though not Christian by tradition, they each exemplify a profound connection to the Divine—what we might call the "Christ Presence." Their lives are living testaments to God's work outside the established borders of Christianity. Even esteemed Christian leaders like Dr. Howard Washington Thurman, Dr. Martin Luther King, Jr., and Archbishop Desmond Tutu have recognized this, offering their voices as credible Christian witnesses to the divine qualities present in these interfaith leaders despite their different religious paths.

As inclusive ministers and laypeople, we must be willing to share our personal experiences of encountering God in unexpected places, sometimes outside the confines of our own faith. We must be willing to find God beyond the familiar. We should ask the tough questions: *Could someone like Gandhi, who lived a life of peace and love, truly be condemned because he was not a Christian? And what about those around us who show love and compassion in ways beyond the traditional Christian mold? What about our neighbors and co-workers who demonstrate the presence of love and goodwill, even though they may worship differently?*

By embracing these experiences, we acknowledge God's presence is not limited by tradition. We affirm the message of love and divine presence is alive, dynamic, and often found where we least expect it. These questions compel us to rethink how we define divine encounters. Tradition is valuable, but experience—when lived and shared—offers a more expansive understanding of God's presence.

YOUR *LifeWork*

Message: As a minister or a layperson, embrace the theme of "Finding and Living God's Presence Across Boundaries." This involves recognizing and celebrating the Divine presence in all faiths, understanding God's love transcends traditional religious boundaries. Drawing inspiration from figures like Gandhi, Thich Nhat Hanh, the Dalai Lama, Dr. Howard Washington Thurman, Dr. Martin Luther King, Jr., and Archbishop Desmond Tutu, explore how God's presence is evident beyond Christianity, and how breaking free from rigid boundaries allows for a more profound encounter with the Divine.

Implementation:

- *Organize an After-Service Series on World Religions*: Once or twice a month, focus on the spiritual practices and teachings of a different faith, highlighting how elements of God's love, peace, and justice are reflected in these traditions and drawing parallels to Christian values.
- *Host an Interfaith Panel Discussion*: Invite representatives from different faith traditions to your faith community to share their experiences of encountering God, fostering mutual understanding and respect.
- *Create a Personal Testimony Night*: Encourage members to share their stories of encountering God in non-traditional ways or through interactions with people of different faiths, and reflect on how these experiences have shaped their understanding of God's presence in the world.

- *Host a Faith Exploration Workshop*: Encourage members to learn about religious traditions outside of Christianity, fostering curiosity and deeper understanding of the Divine in different contexts. Provide a safe space for members to discuss their experiences of God's presence in unexpected places or through interactions with people of different faiths.

Reflection Exercise: As a minister or a layperson, ask yourself these questions: *How does acknowledging God's work in other religions challenge my understanding of faith? When have I felt God's presence in a situation beyond my traditional Christian teachings? How do I express God's love to those who do not share my faith? How can I become more open to experiencing God in unexpected places or people? What religious traditions outside of Christianity have I explored or am curious about? How can I integrate the understanding of God's universal presence into my ministry or personal spiritual practice?* Then consider when it makes sense to ask members these same questions.

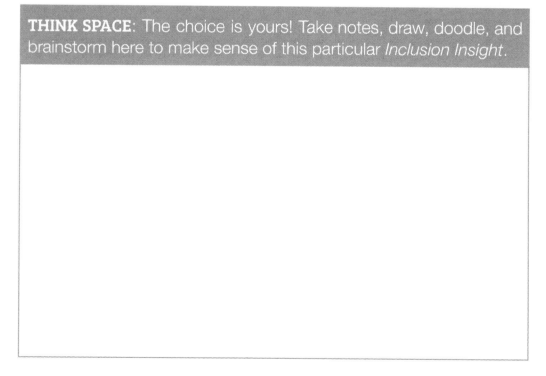

THINK SPACE: The choice is yours! Take notes, draw, doodle, and brainstorm here to make sense of this particular *Inclusion Insight*.

Prayer: "Eternal Mystery, thank You for freeing me from the bondage of my past. Strengthen me to walk into freedom. Amen."

— D.E. Paulk and LaDonna Paulk Diaz
from *Fully Awake 365* (2022)

RITUALS REIMAGINED:
KEEPING TRADITIONS ALIVE

Ritual is the heartbeat of every religious community. They have the power to first connect us to the Divine. Rituals are familiar, comforting, and meaningful. As we embrace inclusion, we must ensure these rituals, reimagined with purpose, continue to serve as bridges between our souls and the Divine presence in worship.

As you transition from a traditional Christian church to an inclusive, interfaith space, it is not the time to discard rituals but to breathe new life into them. Altar calls, for instance, have been central to our tradition. Instead of letting them fade away, we can invite people to experience peace with God, recognizing God has already extended peace to them. This subtle shift in focus preserves the practice while expanding its meaning.

The act of prayer itself can also be reimagined. Rather than adhering strictly to one format, we can invite prayers reflecting a variety of beliefs—whether addressed to God, the universe, or simply spoken from the heart. This approach allows everyone to feel seen and heard, fostering a sense of belonging in our shared worship space.

Tithing is another practice worth retaining, but with a reimagined perspective. No longer should it be tied to fear, obligation, or transactional thinking. Instead, let it flow from a place of gratitude, an expression of appreciation for the abundance we've already received. By transforming its intent, we honor the tradition while opening it up to a broader understanding.

Even water baptism, a profound ritual of faith, can find new expression in this inclusive space. Rather than viewing it solely as a cleansing rite, we can teach it as a symbolic death to ego and a spiritual resurrection into a higher consciousness. By reinterpreting its significance, we maintain its sacredness while making it relevant to all.

Worship, traditionally rooted in singing hymns and reciting scriptures, can evolve into a more expansive expression honoring diverse spiritual journeys. Instead of limiting worship to familiar songs and prayers, we can incorporate music, readings, and meditations from various traditions. This doesn't mean discarding our cherished hymns or scriptures, but complementing them with voices resonating with the broader spiritual community. In doing so, we create a worship experience that is not only inclusive but also deeply enriching for all participants.

YOUR *LifeWork*

Message: As a minister or a layperson, consider how incorporating and redefining diverse spiritual practices can enrich and deepen the worship experience for all participants. By blending elements from various spiritual traditions, you can introduce your members to readings, prayers, and rituals that reflect a more inclusive, interfaith approach. Explore the universality of spiritual practices such as prayer, and examine how these practices can be transformed to resonate with a broader congregation, reflecting universal spiritual truths.

Implementation:

- *Conduct a Prayer and Ritual Workshop*: Guide your community through various forms of prayer and sacred rituals from different traditions. Discuss the symbolism behind these practices and how they can be reinterpreted to align with an inclusive spiritual philosophy.
- *Facilitate a Discussion on Gratitude and Giving*: Lead a session exploring the role of gratitude in spiritual giving, particularly in tithing. Emphasize the shift from giving out of obligation to giving as an expression of thankfulness and abundance.
- *Create a Reflective Meditation Series*: Develop a series of guided meditations incorporating diverse spiritual perspectives. Encourage participants to reflect on how these meditations influence their personal connection with the Divine.

- *Invite Testimonies on Ritual Reinterpretation*: Encourage members to share their experiences of traditional rituals and how these practices have been redefined or transformed to better resonate with their spiritual journey.

Reflection Exercise: As a minister or a layperson, ask yourself these questions: *What new insights did I gain about spiritual practices from exploring diverse traditions? How has my understanding of sacred rituals evolved through this experience? How does viewing tithing and other forms of giving as acts of gratitude change my perspective on these practices? What challenges do I anticipate in integrating and redefining diverse spiritual elements within our worship community? How do I feel about the balance between retaining traditional practices and embracing new, inclusive elements in worship?* Then consider when it makes sense to ask members these same questions.

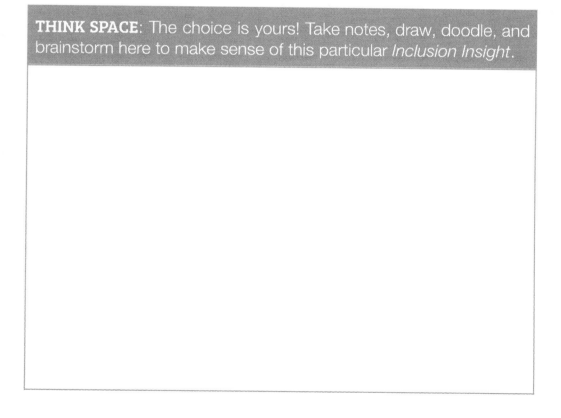

THINK SPACE: The choice is yours! Take notes, draw, doodle, and brainstorm here to make sense of this particular *Inclusion Insight*.

Affirmation: "I set my intention to be spiritual, not religious. Therefore, I will walk in a spirit of love with the desire to restore others."

— D.E. Paulk and LaDonna Paulk Diaz
from *Fully Awake 365* (2022)

LET'S GET ECUMENICAL:
EMBRACING ALL FAITHS

Along my Inclusion Journey towards building a more welcoming faith community, I've come to realize the traditional understanding of ecumenism—typically limited to different Christian denominations—needs to be expanded. To truly embrace the diversity of God's creation, ecumenism must go beyond Christian boundaries and reach out to all religions and philosophies that resonate with the higher ideals of love and neighborly care. In an inclusive religious context, ecumenism expands to encompass inter-religious connections, embracing all of God's children, regardless of their faith tradition.

I've learned that one of the most powerful ways to foster this inclusive mindset is to draw connections between the teachings and wisdom of various religious figures. For instance, the Dalai Lama once said, "My religion is very simple. My religion is kindness" (1998). I see a clear parallel to the message of Jesus in the parable of the Good Samaritan. Here, kindness is extended across cultural and religious lines, highlighting a shared value that transcends any one tradition. This comparison helps to show—while our religions may be distinct—underlying principles of compassion and care are often universal (Doniger, 1998).

I've learned this comparative approach requires sensitivity. It's tempting to lump all religions together under a single umbrella of universal truths, but doing so risks overlooking the unique aspects of each tradition. Instead, I've found it more meaningful to respect these differences while still celebrating the common threads uniting us. This way, we avoid reducing the richness of any one religion and instead create a space where the diversity of beliefs is honored and appreciated (Roberts, 2018).

Incorporating this inclusive mindset into our faith practices involves drawing on the familiar to introduce the unfamiliar. For instance, in the Bible, Jesus speaks of "other sheep that are not of this fold" (The Holy Bible, New King James Version, John 10:16). This passage has become a powerful reminder for me that the universal body of Christ is not confined to just one group. By acknowledging these "other folds" without any intention of converting them, but rather recognizing their place in the broader spiritual family, we open the door to genuine inter-religious dialogue. We can foster a sense of unity without the pressure of conversion, but rather with the intent of reconnection.

Models like the framework found in *Neighbors: Christians and Muslims Building Community* have been instrumental (Womack, 2020). Such models advocate for an interreligious awareness allowing us to engage with different faiths while maintaining our own religious identity. Such models are about understanding and respecting others, not about losing ourselves in the process. The focus shifts from conversion to connection, from division to dialogue, as we seek to learn from each other in a spirit of mutual respect and shared humanity. It's a delicate balance, but one that can help comfort those who might be hesitant about interfaith engagement. In this inclusive vision of faith, the goal is not to convert, but to learn, to grow, and to find common ground in our shared humanity.

YOUR *LifeWork*

Message: As a minister or a layperson, embrace and promote an inclusive vision of ecumenism that transcends denominational and religious boundaries. Foster genuine inter-religious dialogue, build bridges of understanding, and highlight shared values like love and compassion, while respecting the uniqueness of each faith tradition.

Implementation:
- *Create a Comparative Teaching Series*: Develop a series of lessons or sermons that draw connections between the teachings of Jesus and those of other religious figures like the Dalai Lama,

Gandhi, or Muhammad. Highlight both the similarities and the unique aspects of each tradition.

- *Incorporate Interfaith Prayers in Worship*: Introduce prayers or meditative readings from various religious traditions into your services or gatherings. Create a guide that includes prayers, readings, and practices from various faith traditions, along with guidelines for respectful interfaith dialogue and interaction. This can be a way to honor the diversity of faiths while finding common spiritual ground.
- *Encourage Congregational Book Studies*: Choose books exploring interfaith themes or presenting multiple religious perspectives on a common topic. Encourage group discussions that focus on understanding and respecting different viewpoints.

Reflection Exercise: As a minister or a layperson, ask yourself these questions: *What common values do I share with people of other faiths, and how can I highlight these in my interactions? In what ways have I unconsciously imposed my religious views on others, and how can I become more respectful of their beliefs? How can I incorporate teachings from other religions into my spiritual practice in a way that enriches my faith? What steps can I take to build genuine relationships with people from different religious backgrounds? How can I help my congregation appreciate the diversity of religious experiences without feeling threatened by it? What are the potential challenges of interfaith engagement, and how can I address them with sensitivity and care?* Then consider when it makes sense to ask members these same questions.

THINK SPACE: The choice is yours! Take notes, draw, doodle, and brainstorm here to make sense of this particular *Inclusion Insight*.

Affirmation: "I am open and available to see a bigger vision and version of the awesome God of the universe. God is neither male, nor female. God is Spirit. And today, I will worship in spirit and in truth."

— D.E. Paulk and LaDonna Paulk Diaz
from *Fully Awake 365* (2022)

GETTING THERE PA(CE)TIENTLY

I will never forget Easter Sunday morning, 2006. That morning, I delivered a sermon unlike any I had given before. I took the risk of introducing my congregation to other religious figures who had also experienced miraculous resurrections similar to Jesus of Nazareth. My intention was simple, yet profound: to broaden their perspective, to help them see a more expansive view of the Divine, one transcending the boundaries of a single faith tradition.

As I spoke of Krishna and Mithras, whose resurrections predated that of Jesus, I could feel the tension in the air. The silence following was deafening, a stark contrast to the usual affirmations and amens punctuating our services. At that moment, I knew I had to pivot. I shifted the focus back to Jesus, making him the centerpiece of my message once again. It was a necessary move. Jesus needed to remain the central figure, especially on Easter Sunday. I realized pushing too hard, too fast, could potentially alienate the very people I was trying to guide toward a more inclusive understanding of God. Nearly two decades later, I see the fruits of my cautious approach. My congregation has grown more open, more willing to explore interfaith savior characters and disparate holy texts. Yet, their connection to Jesus has not diminished; if anything, it has deepened, now encompassing a wider understanding of God's presence in all of creation.

The lesson I learned that day was invaluable. Change is indeed the only constant in the universe, but it must happen at its own pace. We cannot force it, nor should we try. Instead, we must gently plant seeds, offering new ideas as food for thought, but never demanding they be accepted or understood on our timeline. By creating a safe space where people feel unjudged and in control of their own spiritual journeys, we allow them to discover the truth in their own time, in their own way.

As we move forward in our Inclusion Journey, it is crucial to remember we are not here to convert or even to convince. Conversion is the old way; conversation is the new. Our role is not to teach, but to remove the obstacles preventing people from seeing what they already know deep within: God is bigger than religion, God is in all of creation, and religion is merely a human attempt to define and connect with the Divine. Let us, therefore, be patient, allowing space for growth and change, letting it breathe, and letting it be.

YOUR *LifeWork*

Message: As a minister or a layperson, foster a gradual, inclusive, and non-demanding approach to introducing new, interreligious ideas within your spiritual community. Create a safe and open environment where individuals can explore and expand their understanding of the Divine at their own pace, without feeling pressured or judged.

Implementation:

- *Facilitate Open Dialogue*: Organize small group discussions or study sessions where participants are encouraged to share their thoughts on interreligious concepts.
- *Model Patience in Change*: Demonstrate through your actions and words your respect for each individual's journey and pace of spiritual growth. Publicly acknowledge everyone is on their own path and that it's okay for their understanding to evolve over time.
- *Create a Safe Space*: Ensure your church or spiritual community is a place where people feel comfortable expressing doubts, questions, and new ideas. Encourage leaders and members alike to listen more than they speak, fostering an environment of mutual respect and curiosity.
- *Avoid the Rhetoric of Conversion*: In your teachings and interactions, steer clear of language implying the need to convert others to your way of thinking, whether about Christianity or

inclusion. Instead, focus on sharing experiences and insights inviting others into a broader conversation.

Reflection Exercise: As a minister or a layperson, ask yourself these questions: *How comfortable am I with the idea of integrating teachings from other religious traditions into my own spiritual practice? In what ways can I introduce new ideas to my faith community without overwhelming or alienating them? What steps can I take to shift from a mindset of conversion to one of conversation within my spiritual community? How can I balance the introduction of interreligious ideas with the maintenance of core Christian beliefs? What obstacles do I need to remove to help others see and embrace a more inclusive view of God? How can I model patience and understanding as members of my congregation navigates their own journeys of spiritual growth?* Then consider when it makes sense to ask members these same questions.

THINK SPACE: The choice is yours! Take notes, draw, doodle, and brainstorm here to make sense of this particular *Inclusion Insight.*

Prayer: "Sustainer God, teach me the ways of balance. Give me the passion and pace, the wisdom and way, to endure to the end. Amen."

— D.E. Paulk and LaDonna Paulk Diaz
from *Fully Awake 365* (2022)

IN TUNE: ALIGNING MUSIC WITH THE MESSAGE

In my journey as a spiritual leader, I've come to realize music is far more than just melody and rhythm; it is a conduit for conveying our deepest beliefs and theological understandings. As our understanding of the Divine grows and shifts, so too must the songs carrying our prayers, praises, and reflections. This has been a challenging but necessary realization, one that has called me to reassess the lyrical content of the songs we sing in our sacred spaces.

Over time, I've noticed certain lyrics no longer align with our community's emerging theological perspective. This realization was difficult to accept at first, given the deep emotional connections many of us have with these songs. However, as our awareness of God and ourselves continues to expand, it becomes clear some of these cherished songs must either be revised or retired. It's not just about the melody or the emotion a song invokes; it's about the message it sends. They simply do not reflect the God we now know or the Divine essence we see within ourselves.

Yet, all is not lost. I've learned this need for change doesn't mean we have to discard everything. There is room for adaptation and growth. Many songs can be salvaged by thoughtfully reworking the lyrics to better align with our current beliefs. This process is not just a practical necessity; it is an opportunity for spiritual education. By revising lyrics, we demonstrate that our theology is living and dynamic, and our worship practices should reflect this evolution.

I remember a particular moment at Spirit & Truth Sanctuary when we faced this very challenge. We sing *Welcome Into This Place* (Crouch and Oliver, 1987), a beautiful song long a part of our worship. The original lyrics say, "welcome into this broken vessel." As we began to embrace a more affirming view of our divine nature, the word "broken" no longer felt appropriate. We chose to change the words to "welcome into this open vessel" and this small adjustment became a profound teachable moment. It allowed us to reinforce the idea that we are not broken beings in need of fixing; we are open vessels ready to receive and express the Divine.

Another song in our repertoire repeatedly declares, "He is God" and while the song is beloved, its exclusive use of masculine pronouns does not encompass the fullness of our understanding of God as beyond gender. To address this, I began to add a reflective moment after the song, where I would say, "He is God. She is God. We are God. It is God." This simple expansion honored the original sentiment of the song while inviting the congregation to embrace a broader, more inclusive view of the Divine.

These moments have taught me music in worship is not static. It should evolve alongside our theology. By being willing to adjust and reinterpret lyrics, we not only preserve the beauty and familiarity of beloved songs; we also use them as powerful tools for spiritual growth and understanding.

YOUR *LifeWork*

Message: As a minister or a layperson, recognize the powerful role music plays in shaping and reflecting our theological beliefs. The music we choose and the lyrics we sing should align with our evolving understanding of the Divine and ourselves. Embrace the opportunity to rework, revise, or retire songs no longer aligned with your current theology, using these changes as moments of teaching and spiritual growth within your community.

Implementation:

- *Engage Your Music Team to Review Your Worship Music*: Collaborate with your music team to discuss any potential changes to the lyrics of songs. Encourage open dialogue about the theological implications of the lyrics and the importance of aligning them with your current beliefs. Take time to evaluate the songs currently used in your worship services. Identify any lyrics no longer reflecting your community's evolving theology or understanding of God.

- *Rework Lyrics Thoughtfully and Use Revisions as Teachable Moments:* For songs holding sentimental value but containing problematic lyrics, work together to revise them. Make these changes in a way that preserves the song's essence while bringing it into alignment with your theology. During worship services, take the opportunity to explain why certain lyrics have been changed. Use this as a teaching moment to communicate your community's evolving understanding of the Divine and the importance of inclusive, affirming language.
- *Introduce New Songs Carefully and Encourage Congregational Feedback*: When introducing new songs to your congregation, ensure the lyrics fully reflect your community's current theological stance. Invite feedback from the congregation about the music used in worship. Encourage members to share how the lyrics resonate with their personal understanding of God and spirituality.
- *Create a Worship Music Protocol or Policy*: Develop a clear policy or guideline for selecting worship music aligned with your theology. This can serve as a helpful resource for your music team and anyone involved in planning worship services.

Reflection Exercise: As a minister or a layperson, ask yourself these questions: *How do the current lyrics of our worship songs align with my personal understanding of God and the Divine? Are there any songs in our worship services which no longer resonate with our community's evolving theology? How can I use the revision or reworking of song lyrics as a moment to teach and communicate our community's beliefs? In what ways can we involve the congregation in the process of evaluating and selecting worship music? What steps can I take to ensure new worship songs introduced to our community align with our current beliefs?* Then consider when it makes sense to ask members these same questions.

Affirmation: "I will press into the new and press away from the old. I will surrender my old, lower thinking to new, higher concepts."

— D.E. Paulk and LaDonna Paulk Diaz
from *Fully Awake 365* (2022)

COLLABORATE WITH CO-CREATORS

The journey toward true inclusion isn't one to be traveled alone. Early on, I realized the importance of finding allies—architects of change—who could help shape and solidify the vision of an inclusive community. One of my first steps was to seek out strong, confident cisgender heterosexual men who were secure in their identity. Their presence and strength were not just symbolic; they were vital in bridging gaps often existing between different groups. By appealing to their sense of masculinity, strength, and love, I was able to engage them in a meaningful way, encouraging them to use their influence to support this vision of inclusion.

In addition to these men, I connected with successful cisgender heterosexual women who had the clarity of vision to see where we were headed. These women were not only confident but also strategic thinkers, capable of understanding the long-term impact of our efforts. Their involvement added a crucial dimension to our collective endeavor.

The collaboration didn't stop there; the LGBTQ+ community was another cornerstone of our efforts. I also reached out to cisgender and transgender LGBTQ+ individuals who were comfortable in their own skin, compassionate, and patient. Their willingness to engage with those who might still be grappling with old prejudices and misconceptions was crucial. They handled ignorant questions and offensive language with grace, educating and enlightening rather than alienating.

As we worked together, I made it clear this journey would require patience and understanding. Many people were in the process of shedding old religious conditioning and cultural biases, and I knew they needed time and grace to fully embrace a new consciousness. I articulated this vision to my group of co-creators, emphasizing the importance of unity and inclusion.

This approach was intentional, designed to avoid the creation of yet another segregated group. While I deeply respect the role LGBTQ+ churches have played in providing safe spaces, my vision was to go a step further—to build a truly inclusive community that embraced all people. This has meant finding, building, and nourishing a tribe of individuals who were committed to this shared vision. Together, we could create something that was not only inclusive but also enduring and transformative.

YOUR *LifeWork*
Message: As a minister or a layperson, actively seek out and collaborate with individuals who can help you build an inclusive community. This means engaging with people of diverse backgrounds, including those who are confident in their identities and committed to the vision of inclusion.

Implementation:
- *Identify Allies*: Begin by identifying strong, confident people within your community who are secure in their identities. Approach them with a clear vision of what inclusion means and how they can contribute.
- *Provide Educational Materials*: Create or source educational materials addressing common misconceptions and biases related to gender, sexuality, and inclusion. Use these materials to train your community leaders and members.
- *Build Cross-Group Relationships*: Facilitate activities or programs to bring together people from different backgrounds to work on projects or causes. This helps to build understanding and camaraderie among diverse groups.
- *Develop Inclusivity Guidelines*: Work with your co-creators to develop clear guidelines or a mission statement reflecting your community's commitment to inclusion. Ensure these guidelines are communicated clearly and regularly to all members.

- *Provide Ongoing Support*: Offer ongoing support and resources for those who are still adjusting to a more inclusive environment. This might include counseling, peer support groups, or additional training.
- *Celebrate Diversity*: Organize events celebrating the diversity within your community. This could include cultural festivals, Pride events, or simply recognition of various heritage months.

Reflection Exercise: As a minister or a layperson, ask yourself these questions: *Who in my community are the natural leaders I can engage to support our inclusion efforts? Am I providing enough opportunities for diverse voices to be heard? What biases might I still hold, and how can I work to overcome them? What steps am I taking to ensure my community is not just inclusive in name but in practice? How can I support members of my community who are still grappling with old biases?* Then consider when it makes sense to ask members these same questions.

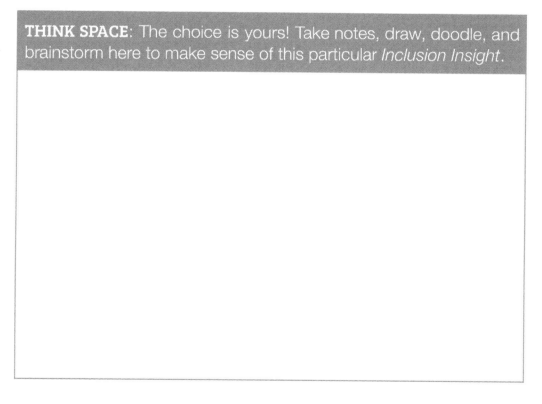

THINK SPACE: The choice is yours! Take notes, draw, doodle, and brainstorm here to make sense of this particular *Inclusion Insight*.

Prayer: "Authentic Spirit, grant me the courage to be vulnerable, the compassion to be empathetic, and the candor to connect. Amen."

— D.E. Paulk and LaDonna Paulk Diaz
from *Fully Awake 365* (2022)

METHOD OVER THE MADNESS OF MODALITY

When I was eight years old, I had an experience that forever changed my understanding of the Divine. It was during a Christian worship service, and as the congregation sang and prayed, I felt something shift deep within me. The Holy Ghost fell upon me, and suddenly, I was speaking in tongues. The experience was overwhelming; I was in a trance, lost in a language not my own, yet it felt as though it was coming from the very core of my being. The joy was indescribable, and the presence of God's love was so tangible I could almost touch it.

For years, I held onto this experience as evidence of the truth of my religion. It seemed to prove Christianity was the ultimate way to connect with the Divine. But as I grew older and began to explore other spiritual traditions, I encountered similar experiences in contexts far removed from my own. I realized my experience was not unique to Christianity.

Thirty years after my first experience, I attended a traditional Hindu celebration of Ganesha Puja. As the rituals unfolded, I felt a familiar shift within me. The Holy Ghost, or perhaps simply the presence of the Divine, fell upon me again. It was the same overwhelming presence of the Divine I'd felt in my childhood. Tears streamed down my face, my tongue quivered, and I felt those same chills and overwhelming joy. It was as if the veil between the physical and spiritual worlds had been lifted. I was once again in the presence of God's boundless love.

This experience challenged everything I had believed about the exclusive truth of my religion. It showed me that the modality—the specific practices and beliefs of a religion—is not the most important thing. What truly matters is the broader methodology, the deeper, underlying desire for connection with the Divine. Whether through Christian worship, the whirling of dervishes in Islam, the transcendent dances of American Native spirituality, or even the placebo effect of believing in healing, these are all different paths leading to the same ultimate goal…connection.

As I reflected on these experiences, I began to share them with my church, encouraging a more expansive view of God transcending the limitations of any single religious framework (Elkins, 1998). I began to encourage a broader vision of God, one not limited to a single modality. It's important to recognize while our experiences within a specific religious framework can be deeply meaningful, they are not the only way to connect with the Divine. The constant in all of this is the perceiver—the individual seeking connection, not the particular modality they use to achieve it.

The truth, as I have come to understand it, is beautifully captured in the words of Emmet Fox, "The whole outer world...is amenable to man's thought, and that he has dominion over it when he knows it." (1938). Our thoughts, beliefs, and experiences shape our connection to the Divine, and in that, we find our true power. The methodology remains the pursuit of this connection, while the modalities are simply the varied expressions of that pursuit.

YOUR *LifeWork*

Message: As a minister or a layperson, recognize the pursuit of a divine connection transcends any single religious framework or modality. The true essence lies in the methodology—the deeper, universal quest for connection with God—rather than in the specific practices or beliefs shaping our individual experiences. Focus on broadening your understanding of spirituality by exploring and appreciating the diverse ways in which people connect with the Divine across different traditions and modalities.

Implementation:

- *Use Other Spiritual Practices*: Attend a religious service or spiritual gathering outside of your own tradition, such as a meditation session, a Sufi whirling ceremony, or a Native

American spiritual ritual. Reflect on the similarities and differences in how people experience the Divine.

- *Teach the Concept of Modality vs. Methodology*: In your next sermon, Bible study, or small group session, introduce the idea that while our religious practices (modalities) are meaningful, they are not the only paths to God. Emphasize the importance of the underlying methodology—the desire to connect with the Divine.
- *Share Personal Experiences and Encourage Exploration*: Share your own spiritual experiences, especially those occurring outside of your primary religious tradition. Encourage others to share their experiences as well, fostering an environment of openness and acceptance. Invite your congregation or group members to explore a spiritual practice or tradition they are unfamiliar with.
- *Study and Reflect*: Lead a study group on the works of authors like Emmet Fox and other spiritual thinkers who discuss the universality of spiritual experiences. Discuss how these ideas can be integrated into your own faith practice.

Reflection Exercise: As a minister or a layperson, ask yourself these questions: *Have I experienced a connection with the Divine outside of my primary religious tradition? If so, how did it compare to my experiences within my tradition? How do I perceive other religions or spiritual practices? How can I encourage others in my community to explore and appreciate different spiritual traditions without feeling threatened? What steps can I take to foster a spirit of unity and mutual respect among people of different faiths within my community?* Then consider when it makes sense to ask members these same questions.

THINK SPACE: The choice is yours! Take notes, draw, doodle, and brainstorm here to make sense of this particular *Inclusion Insight*.

Affirmation: "I am stronger because of the many voices I have heard, places I have gone, and people I have encountered. This wealth of diversity will guide me, inform me, and keep me safe."

— D.E. Paulk and LaDonna Paulk Diaz
from *Fully Awake 365* (2022)

SEE THE BIG PICTURE: VISUAL INCLUSIVITY

When I first encountered the idea of visual inclusivity, it was both challenging and enlightening. I've always understood most people are visual learners, myself included. Images have the power to evoke deep emotions, summon memories, and convey complex ideas in ways words often cannot. I've also learned unfamiliar images can evoke fear, especially when they clash with deeply ingrained religious teachings. There was a time when unfamiliar images felt uncomfortable, even threatening, especially given my religious upbringing.

I remember the first time I came across the depiction of El Shaddai, described as the many-breasted God. This image, which symbolizes the nurturing essence of God, was startling to me at first. It was so different from the more traditional images of God I had been conditioned to accept—God as a wise old white-bearded white man, a fatherly figure, strong and protective. Yet, as I allowed myself to dwell on the symbolism, I realized how this image resonated with the idea of God as a nurturer, constantly giving and sustaining life. The many breasts were not strange or perverse; they were a powerful representation of abundance and care.

In contrast, my reaction to images from other religions, like the multi-armed deities of Hinduism, was different. These images didn't evoke the same immediate sense of comfort. Instead, they felt foreign, even unsettling. This reaction was rooted in my religious background, where such images were often seen as strange, labeled as false gods, or even worse, demonic. When I compared this to my reaction to the many-breasted El Shaddai, I had to ask myself: *Why does one seem familiar and the other so foreign? Does God truly prefer breasts to arms?* I had to confront an uncomfortable truth in my answer: my discomfort wasn't about the images themselves but about my conditioned responses to what was unfamiliar.

The question extended further when considering the imagery in the books of Daniel and John—creatures with multiple heads, each symbolizing different aspects of God's creation. Because these were part of my religious tradition, they didn't evoke the same discomfort as the Hindu deity Ganesha, with Its elephant head. In truth, they were not so different. They were all cultural attempts to capture the Divine in ways transcending human form and function.

As I've continued to explore these questions, I've come to see the importance of visual inclusivity in fostering a truly interfaith community. It's not enough to simply tolerate different images; we must seek to understand them, to find the Divine in the unfamiliar. The Holy Spirit has been a guiding presence in this journey, helping me to approach these images with an open heart and mind. By embracing visual inclusivity, I'm learning to see the big picture, to appreciate the diverse ways in which different cultures and religions depict the Divine. This has enriched my faith and broadened my understanding of what it means to be part of a global, interfaith, inclusive, spiritual community.

YOUR *LifeWork*

Message: As a minister or a layperson, embrace and promote visual inclusivity within your faith community. Challenge yourself and others to broaden the understanding of divine imagery by exploring and appreciating representations of the Divine from different cultures and religions. Foster an interfaith community grounded in respect, understanding, and inclusion.

Implementation:

- *Introduce Diverse Visuals in Worship*: Incorporate a variety of religious images from different faith traditions into your worship space, sermons, or presentations. Explain the significance of each image and how it represents aspects of the Divine.
- *Organize an Interfaith Exhibit and Artist Talk*: Collaborate with local artists from various religious backgrounds to create an art exhibit showcasing diverse depictions of the Divine. Encourage

attendees to engage with the art and explore the meanings behind the images. Facilitate an artist talk focused on visual representations of the Divine across different religions. Use this as an opportunity to educate your community about the symbolism in these images and to address any discomfort they might feel.

- *Create a Visual Meditation Practice*: Develop a meditation or prayer practice centered around contemplating different religious images. Encourage participants to reflect on what each image evokes and how it might expand their understanding of the Divine.
- *Offer a Workshop on Symbolism in Religious Art*: Organize a workshop that dives into the symbolism found in religious art from various traditions. Focus on how these symbols convey deeper spiritual truths and how they can enrich one's own faith journey.

Reflection Exercise: As a minister or a layperson, ask yourself these questions: *How do I react to religious images unfamiliar to me, and why do I think that is? What can I learn from the symbols and images of the Divine in other religions? Have I ever dismissed or demonized an image because it was unfamiliar? What does doing so say about my own biases? In what ways can diverse visual representations of the Divine enhance my own spiritual journey? How does my faith tradition's imagery influence my perception of God? How could that perception be broadened? What steps can I take to ensure that my community is more visually inclusive and appreciative of different religious traditions?* Then consider when it makes sense to ask members these same questions.

THINK SPACE: The choice is yours! Take notes, draw, doodle, and brainstorm here to make sense of this particular *Inclusion Insight*.

Prayer: "Creator of Diversity, I am grateful for the diverse people, places and experiences You bring my way. They make me stronger. Amen."

— D.E. Paulk and LaDonna Paulk Diaz
from *Fully Awake 365* (2022)

NAVIGATING CHANGE WITH CARE

I've always believed the heartbeat of our church isn't just in the sermons or the services—it's in the personal connections we build with each member. I was reminded of this one day when I noticed a change in our financial reports. A key contributor had stopped giving, and while it could have been for any number of reasons, I knew it was important to find out why.

One thing I've learned over the years is that body language and outward expressions both can be deceiving. Each person in our congregation brings their own story, their own set of challenges, and their own way of expressing themselves. Some wear their hearts on their sleeves, while others might seem distant or disengaged, even when they're deeply involved. It can be easy to misread these cues, which is why I've found it crucial to reach out, to get personal.

When I called this particular member, my approach was simple and non-intrusive. I didn't want them to feel like I was keeping tabs on their contributions; instead, I wanted them to know I genuinely cared about how they were doing. "I know we've been introducing some new concepts lately," I said. "How are you feeling about everything? Is there anything you'd like to discuss?"

Opening up these lines of communication has proven to be vital in our church's Inclusion Journey. These conversations can be delicate, but they're necessary. It's not just about keeping people from leaving; it's about fostering an environment where they feel safe to express their concerns and questions. I've found when members feel heard, they're more likely to stay engaged, even if they're wrestling with the changes we're implementing.

I've also had to remind myself—and sometimes our leadership team—there's no shame in being aware of our members' giving patterns. Yes, church isn't a business in the traditional sense, but we do have responsibilities, and we can't ignore the financial aspects of keeping our mission going. We have bills to pay, programs to support, and a community to serve. When someone who has been a generous giver starts to struggle, it's a sign to lean in, not back away. Not to judge, but to understand and support them when they're going through tough times.

I've made it a practice to meet with our big givers and, really, all our givers, one by one. It's not about making them feel singled out. It's about understanding their journey and being there for them, especially when they're feeling uneasy. It's in these personal meetings that I've been able to address concerns, offer clarity, and most importantly, remind them their voice matters in our community.

These one-on-one conversations have been some of the most impactful moments in my ministry. Such conversations are about more than money—they're about connection and trust. They've allowed me to connect on a deeper level, to address concerns head-on, and to ensure our church remains a place of support and community, even as we navigate the complexities of change.

YOUR *LifeWork*
Message: As a minister or a layperson, your role in fostering inclusion within the church involves personal connections beyond public worship or teachings. By reaching out to individuals, especially during times of change or financial shifts, you ensure every member feels valued, heard, and supported. Building these one-on-one relationships is crucial for maintaining a cohesive and engaged community, particularly when navigating through periods of significant transformation.

Implementation:
- *Schedule Personal Check-Ins*: As a minister or a layperson, make it a priority to regularly reach out to members, especially those who seem less engaged or have shown changes in their financial contributions. Use these conversations to show genuine care and to listen to their thoughts and concerns.

- *Create an Open Dialogue Environment with a Follow-Up System*: During your one-on-one meetings, use phrases like, "I'm sure you've noticed some changes recently, how are you feeling about everything?" This opens the door for honest dialogue and helps members feel comfortable discussing their concerns or uncertainties. After each personal meeting, create a system to follow up with members, ensuring their concerns are addressed and they feel supported as the church continues to evolve.
- *Support Members*: If you identify members who are struggling, whether financially, emotionally, or spiritually, offer appropriate resources and support. This could include counseling, financial advice, or simply being a listening ear.
- *Acknowledge and Appreciate Contributions*: Regularly express gratitude for the contributions of time, talent, and tithes members make to your faith community. Acknowledgment can go a long way in making individuals feel valued and appreciated.
- *Encourage Leadership Transparency*: Work in partnership with the church leadership team to ensure the reasons behind new changes or initiatives are clearly communicated to all members. Transparency helps in reducing anxiety and increasing trust within the congregation.

Reflection Exercise: As a minister or a layperson, ask yourself these questions: *How often do I personally reach out to members of the congregation to check on their well-being, especially those who seem disengaged or have changed their giving habits? Am I comfortable discussing financial contributions with members, and do I approach these conversations with empathy and care? How do I ensure members feel heard and valued, even when they disagree with new changes or concepts being introduced? How do I respond to signs of distress or disengagement in members? Do I have a plan to offer support? How transparent am I, or the church leadership, about the reasons behind significant changes or initiatives? What follow-up actions do I take after having one-on-one conversations with members to ensure they continue to feel supported?* Then consider when it makes sense to ask members these same questions.

THINK SPACE: The choice is yours! Take notes, draw, doodle, and brainstorm here to make sense of this particular *Inclusion Insight*.

Affirmation: "Through this awakening process I have realized I am not my beliefs. I am a spirit capable of considering, having and even changing beliefs. I am at peace being surrendered to the process of the Holy Spirit guiding me into all truth, even if all truth is different from my present truth."

— D.E. Paulk and LaDonna Paulk Diaz
from *Fully Awake 365* (2022)

THINK GLOBALLY AND ACT LOCALLY

When I first encountered the phrase "Think Globally and Act Locally", it resonated with me in ways I hadn't fully grasped until I began working towards creating a more inclusive faith community (Geddes, 1915). The simplicity of the phrase masks the complexity of its application, particularly when it comes to inclusion. I learned early on that inclusion isn't a one-size-fits-all approach. What works in one context might be completely ineffective in another, and this became strikingly clear as I observed the differences between American and African approaches to inclusion.

In the United States, the approach to inclusion varies dramatically. I found what resonates in a Southern church might feel completely out of place in a Northern or Western congregation. Moreover, the dynamics within predominantly white churches differ from those in predominantly Black churches. I quickly realized even these distinctions are oversimplifications; not all white churches are the same, just as not all Black churches share the same cultural or theological outlook.

When I started engaging with churches across the continent of Africa, it became apparent while they were open to discussing cultural diversity, the topic of LGBTQ+ affirmation was still a sensitive and often avoided subject. Predominantly Latinx churches with which I have engaged were more open to exploring universal salvation but less receptive to questioning rapture theology. These experiences taught me the importance of being acutely aware of the specific cultural and theological contexts I was entering. I learned to avoid overgeneralizing; each congregation had its unique dynamics, shaped by a variety of factors including history, theology, and community culture.

One of the most valuable lessons I learned was the importance of language. Certain words and phrases can unintentionally trigger anxiety or resistance. For instance, in some environments, terms like "inclusive" or "progressive" may be met with suspicion or outright rejection. I had to find ways to frame these conversations to open doors rather than close them. This required a deep understanding of the culture and openness of each environment I was working in.

Ultimately, the goal of inclusion is to stretch minds without shattering them. This means understanding the limits of each community's openness and gently pushing those boundaries without causing harm. I found thinking globally—understanding the broader implications and goals of inclusion—while acting locally—tailoring my approach to the specific community—was essential in making meaningful progress. This insight continues to guide me as I work towards helping others build more inclusive faith communities.

YOUR *LifeWork*
Message: As a minister or a layperson, foster an inclusive faith community by understanding and respecting the unique cultural and theological contexts of each community. The phrase "Think Globally and Act Locally" can guide your efforts as you navigate these differences. Your role is to tailor your approach to inclusion to stretch the minds of your congregation without causing division or harm.

Implementation:
- *Assess Readiness for Difficult Conversations*: Before introducing topics like LGBTQ+ inclusion or critiques of traditional theological views, gauge your community's readiness through surveys, one-on-one conversations, or anonymous feedback channels.
- *Host Community Conversations*: Organize small group discussions within your faith community focusing on the importance of cultural and theological diversity. Encourage participants to share their experiences and perspectives on inclusion.
- *Offer Cultural Sensitivity Training*: Arrange workshops or invite guest speakers to educate your congregation about the cultural and theological differences existing within, between, and among

various communities. This can include understanding how language and symbols are perceived differently in different contexts.

- *Ongoing Education and Reflection*: Encourage continuous learning by suggesting books, podcasts, and articles exploring themes of cultural diversity and inclusion. Create spaces for ongoing reflection and discussion within your community.

Reflection Exercise: As a minister or a layperson, ask yourself these questions: *How well do I understand the cultural and theological diversity within my own faith community? What words or phrases have I used in the past that might unintentionally trigger anxiety or resistance in others? How can I prepare myself to stretch the minds of my congregation without causing harm or division? What specific steps have I taken to educate myself about the cultural and theological differences existing within the broader faith community? What signs or feedback should I look for to assess whether my community is ready for more challenging conversations about inclusion?* Then consider when it makes sense to ask members these same questions.

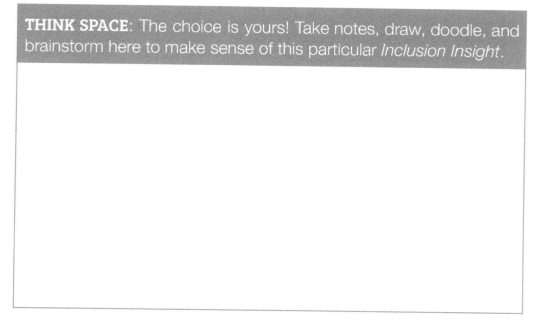

THINK SPACE: The choice is yours! Take notes, draw, doodle, and brainstorm here to make sense of this particular *Inclusion Insight*.

Prayer: "New Mind, grant me a violent spirit to overthrow any thought that keeps me from my highest good and best self. Amen."

— D.E. Paulk and LaDonna Paulk Diaz
from *Fully Awake 365* (2022)

HEAR THEM OUT:
EMBRACE THE CRITICS

Criticism is never easy to swallow, especially when you've poured your heart into something as deeply personal as a sermon. I've always been someone who thrives on positive feedback—those reassuring "amens" and affirming smiles from the congregation. They tell me I'm on the right track, my words are making a difference. But what happens when those affirmations aren't there? When the room is filled with silence or, worse yet, when someone dares to voice a disagreement? For a long time, I shied away from those moments, retreating to the safety of my supporters. But that changed after a particularly eye-opening experience with a Seasoned Saint who sat quietly throughout my sermon. At the end of the service, instead of the usual praise, the elder member approached me with a somber expression and said, "Pastor, I'm not so sure about what you're saying." At first, I felt defensive, tempted to seek the solace of those who support me unconditionally. But something inside urged me to listen, and that moment made *the* difference in my ministry.

Preachers like myself often gravitate toward those who agree with us, those who echo our thoughts and offer the encouragement fueling our passion. It's a natural inclination. We love to be reassured, to hear our words are resonating with our congregation. However, this inclination can lead us away from the people who may be quietly grappling with our messages—those who might be confused, challenged, or even upset by what we preach. These critics—though they may not shower us with praise—represent a significant portion of our community, and they offer an opportunity for growth, both for ourselves and for our ministry.

Some years ago, I partnered with the spiritual leader of a faith community I'll call "United Truth International Center for Living Mindfully and Ecumenically" (UTICLME) to study the attendance and financial contribution patterns of their members. The spiritual leader graciously provided me with a year's worth of data for 40 members, split evenly between two groups: younger, self-proclaimed inclusive-progressives aged 25 to 49, and older, self-professed dogmatic-conservatives aged 50 and above. I was eager to see how these two groups differed in their support of the spiritual center, particularly in light of the congregation's recent shift toward a more inclusive theology.

The results were surprising. The younger, inclusive and progressive members, who had enthusiastically embraced the spiritual center's new direction, attended services less frequently, averaging just 1.3 Sundays each month. Their total financial contributions for the year amounted to $26,874, or an average of $1,343 per person. In contrast, the older, dogmatic and conservative members, who had been more resistant to change, were far more consistent in their attendance, averaging 2.9 Sundays each month. They also contributed significantly more, with a total of $35,748, or about $1,787 per person.

This data challenged many of my assumptions. I had expected the younger, more progressive members to be more engaged and generous, given their excitement about the spiritual center's new direction. Instead, it was the older, more traditional members—those who had initially struggled with the changes—who were the most reliable in their attendance and financial support. These findings forced me to reconsider the dynamics at play within their congregation. From a sociological perspective, I attempted to maintain a non-evaluative intent unconcerned with either judging or rejecting findings as a result of my own cultural filters becoming overtly and subjectively burdensome (Johnson, 1977). The older, conservative members seemed to be driven by a sense of duty, perhaps rooted in a fear of divine retribution or a strict adherence to biblical commands. Verses like Hebrews 10:25, which admonishes believers not to forsake assembling together, and Malachi 3:8-12, which warns against robbing God of tithes and offerings, may have played a significant role in their commitment (The Holy Bible, New King James Version, 1982). In contrast, the younger, progressive members might have been less motivated by fear and more by a sense of personal agency in their spiritual practice. This shift in motivation could explain why they attended less frequently and gave less financially.

My study of UTICLME reminded me to listen to those who challenge me, rather than simply seek out affirmation. The critics in my own congregation, the ones who don't always agree with me or who question my messages, are often the ones who care the most about the future of our faith community. By engaging with them and understanding their concerns, I've been able to strengthen my ministry and build a more inclusive and supportive environment for everyone. Embracing criticism has not only made me a better preacher but has also deepened my connection with my congregation, helping me to serve them more effectively.

In the end, hearing out the critics—those who sit quietly, unsure, or even upset—is crucial. They are the ones who can push us to think more deeply, to question our assumptions, and to grow in ways we never expected. And in doing so, we create a community that is not only more inclusive but also more resilient and enduring.

YOUR *LifeWork*

Message: As a minister or a layperson, listen to those who may not always agree with you. Embracing criticism can lead to deeper insights, stronger relationships, and a more resilient faith community. By engaging with those who challenge your ideas, rather than retreating to the comfort of like-minded individuals, you can foster a more inclusive and dynamic environment that supports the growth and sustainability of your ministry or faith group.

Implementation:

- *Host an All-Church Meeting or Forum*: Organize a gathering at least twice a year where members of your congregation can express their thoughts, concerns, or critiques about recent sermons or church decisions. Ensure this is a safe space for honest dialogue, where every voice is heard and respected.

- *Host Sermon Talk Backs*: After delivering a sermon, host a 30-minute Talk Back session to seek feedback from members who are less vocal or who have previously expressed differing viewpoints. You may also do this through anonymous surveys, suggestion boxes, or personal conversations.
- *Create a Critique Circle*: Develop a small group to discuss theological topics and church practices. Encourage members with varying perspectives to join and participate in regular meetings, fostering an environment of constructive criticism and diverse viewpoints. Many of these topics and ideas could easily be used to craft future sermons.
- *Empower Lay Leaders*: Coach and train lay leaders in the congregation on how to handle and embrace criticism constructively. Equip them with tools and strategies for fostering open, honest discussions within their respective groups or ministries.
- *Encourage Mindful Giving*: Discuss the findings of your research with your congregation, highlighting the different motivations behind attendance and financial contributions. Encourage members to reflect on their own motivations and how they can align their actions with the values they wish to uphold.

Reflection Exercise: As a minister or a layperson, ask yourself these questions: *How do I typically respond to criticism? Do I embrace it, or do I shy away from it? How can I better engage with members who may feel confused or upset by recent changes or messages in the church? What can I learn from the financial and attendance patterns of different groups within my congregation? How does this inform my understanding of their motivations? How can I model the behavior of embracing criticism in my own life, both within the church and in my personal relationships? What steps can I take to ensure my ministry is inclusive of all perspectives, not just those that align with my own beliefs?* Then consider when it makes sense to ask members these same questions.

Affirmation: "I celebrate the BEGINNER'S MIND. I am the knowing and the unknowing. I am believing and disbelieving. I am learning and unlearning. In this present moment I surrender to the process of being transformed by the renewing of my mind."

— D.E. Paulk and LaDonna Paulk Diaz
from *Fully Awake 365* (2022)

ROLL UP YOUR SLEEVES: LEADING BY EXAMPLE

I remember when we first started talking about beginning the Inclusion Journey in our church. It was a new idea, unfamiliar to many, and not everyone was quick to embrace it. I understand people often connect more with the person delivering the message than the message itself. This isn't just a theory to me; it is something I live.

Each week, I spend time doing the manual work around the church—cutting grass, painting walls, blowing leaves, and other tasks. It isn't all that glamorous, but necessary. Over the years, as I have worked with my hands, I have noticed something interesting. There are men in my congregation, who initially did not embrace the message of inclusion. They were skeptical, unsure if this new direction was the right one. They saw me out there, getting dirty, not just preaching about change but living it. My willingness to roll up my sleeves kept them engaged. They didn't buy into the message right away; however, once they connected with my work ethic. This encouraged them to stick around long enough for it to start making sense.

It wasn't just the physical labor that made a difference. My wife and I also made a financial decision which, though unintentional at the time, sent a powerful message. My wife left her full-time job at the church, choosing instead to volunteer while seeking employment in the corporate world. We didn't do this to prove anything to anyone, yet it had a profound impact. Our choice showed the congregation we were committed to the mission, even if it meant making personal sacrifices. This steadied those who were on the fence, unsure if they could trust this new theology of inclusion.

In hindsight, it became clear leading by example wasn't just about what we said but about how we lived our lives. Our character and collective work ethic spoke louder than any sermon could. People are personality-driven, and they need to see the messenger embodying the message. This wasn't about elevating myself or my wife. It was about living such that the message of inclusion was tangible and real for those who were watching. By rolling up our sleeves, both figuratively and literally, we were able to bridge the gap between skepticism and belief, guiding our congregation through a period of change. We were able to create a space where the message could be heard, understood, and ultimately embraced.

YOUR *LifeWork*

Message: As a minister or a layperson, foster trust and commitment within your community. Whether it's through your work ethic, financial decisions, or everyday actions, demonstrating the values you preach can be more impactful than words alone. By embodying the message of inclusion in your daily life, you provide a living example others can follow.

Implementation:
- *Engage in Visible Service*: Participate in hands-on tasks within your community, such as cleaning, organizing, or assisting with events. Make sure these efforts are seen by others to show you are not above any work.
- *Model Financial Responsibility*: Publicly share stories about how you manage your finances to support your community's mission. Consider leading a workshop or discussion on financial stewardship, emphasizing the importance of living beneath your means.
- *Be and Do*: Instead of simply instructing others on how to live out the values of inclusion, demonstrate them through your own actions. For example, if promoting generosity, start by personally contributing time, resources, or money to a community cause. Offer to mentor others in your community, sharing not only advice but also allowing them to witness how you handle challenges and

live out your values. This can be particularly powerful for those who are skeptical or unsure about adopting new practices.

- *Communicate Transparently*: Regularly update your community on your personal and financial commitments to the mission. This transparency builds trust and shows you are fully invested in the same goals you are asking others to support. If possible, involve your family in community service or church activities, demonstrating a collective commitment to the mission. Share your family's journey, including sacrifices or adjustments made, to inspire others.

Reflection Exercise: As a minister or a layperson, ask yourself these questions: *Am I actively demonstrating the values I preach in my daily actions? How do my financial decisions reflect my commitment to the mission of inclusion? What specific examples of service or sacrifice can I share with my community to inspire them? How have I supported or recognized the contributions of others within my community? In what ways can I involve my family or close friends in demonstrating these values? Am I being transparent with my community about the challenges and sacrifices involved in living out these values? How can I mentor or guide others through my example rather than just my words?* Then consider when it makes sense to ask members these same questions.

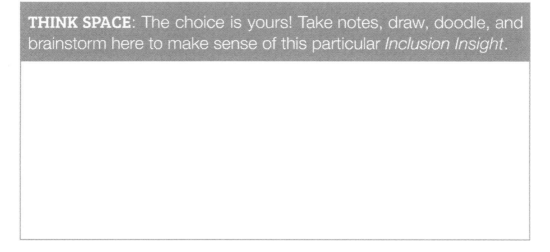

THINK SPACE: The choice is yours! Take notes, draw, doodle, and brainstorm here to make sense of this particular *Inclusion Insight*.

Affirmation: "I will be open to see a different story unfold from the one I expected."

— D.E. Paulk and LaDonna Paulk Diaz
from *Fully Awake 365* (2022)

CONVERSE, DON'T CONVERT:
DIALOGUE OVER DOGMA

Old habits die hard, and this truth became strikingly clear to me as I began teaching about inclusion. I spent years in the realm of Evangelical Christianity, where conversion was the ultimate goal. The belief was deeply ingrained that if you weren't actively converting others, you were somehow falling short. Bishop Pearson would often remind us with his saying, "Converge to Converse, without seeking to Convince or Convert." It was a mantra that sounded progressive, yet its full meaning didn't sink in for me until much later.

About ten years into my work, a revelation struck me. Despite my departure from literal interpretations of scripture, and my conscious rejection of concepts like the devil and hell, I realized I was still trapped in an old modality. I had simply swapped one form of conversion for another. No longer was I trying to convert people to Christianity; instead, I was trying to convert them to inclusion. I was still operating from a mindset seeking to change others, to convince them to see the world as I did. I had unknowingly taken the evangelistic zeal once fueling my efforts to save souls and repurposed it to champion inclusion.

This realization was both humbling and liberating. I recognized I was still pouring new wine into an old wineskin. The language and tactics had changed, but the underlying intent was the same—to convince others of what I believed to be the truth. Once I saw this pattern, I knew it was time to shift my approach. Instead of pushing others toward my conclusions, I started to invite them into a conversation. I began to use phrases like, "Have you ever considered?" and reassured them that "there are no deal breakers here."

This shift wasn't just about adopting a new vocabulary; it was about allowing people the space and grace to process new ideas at their own pace. I realized true inclusion isn't about convincing others to adopt your worldview, but rather about creating a space where diverse perspectives can coexist without the pressure to conform. It was a move away from the urgency to convert and toward the patience to converse. By letting go of the need to convert, I found dialogue flourished, and with it, a deeper understanding and acceptance of inclusion.

YOUR *LifeWork*

Message: As a minister or a layperson, prioritize genuine dialogue over the need to convince or convert others. Create a space where diverse perspectives can be shared freely, allowing others to process new ideas at their own pace without pressure or coercion. This approach fosters an environment of true inclusion and understanding.

Implementation:

- *Host Workshops on Dialogue Techniques*: Offer training sessions on effective communication techniques fostering dialogue, such as active listening, asking open-ended questions, and managing disagreements constructively.
- *Use Invitational Language*: When discussing topics of faith, inclusion, or social issues, deliberately use phrases like, "Have you ever considered?" or "What are your thoughts on...?" to invite conversation rather than impose your views.
- *Model Non-Coercive Leadership*: In your sermons, teachings, or meetings, model the behavior of engaging in dialogue without seeking to convince. Share stories highlighting the importance of understanding different perspectives.
- *Teach the Value of Patience*: Incorporate lessons on the importance of patience in conversations about difficult topics. Emphasize understanding and acceptance often take time and it's okay for people to be at different stages in their journey.

Reflection Exercise: As a minister or a layperson, ask yourself these questions: *How do I approach conversations? With the intention of* understanding, or more focused on convincing others of my point of view, or something else? How often do I use invitational language in discussions, and how does it impact the dialogue? What practices have I put in place to ensure diverse perspectives are respected in group discussions? How do I handle disagreements within my community? Am I comfortable with the idea others may never fully agree with me, and can I still value their perspectives? Then consider when it makes sense to ask members these same questions.

THINK SPACE: The choice is yours! Take notes, draw, doodle, and brainstorm here to make sense of this particular *Inclusion Insight*.

Prayer: "Omnipresent Spirit, I give thanks that You are evenly present in all of creation. I am open to seeing You everywhere. Amen."

— D.E. Paulk and LaDonna Paulk Diaz
from *Fully Awake 365* (2022)

OOPS, MY BAD:
THE POWER OF APOLOGY

There is an undeniable excitement that comes with discovering new insights, especially when those insights expand our understanding of faith and inclusion. I remember the exhilaration I felt as I began to explore the depths of inclusion, delving into texts and teachings from various traditions—Taoism, Hinduism, Buddhism—all of which opened my eyes to the vastness of a God who could not be contained within the pages of a single holy book. This newfound knowledge filled me with a passion to share these revelations with my congregation, eager to take them on the same journey I was experiencing.

However, in my enthusiasm, I failed to notice I was moving too quickly. Week after week, I introduced these new ideas from the pulpit, eager to share the beauty of what I was learning. I was so caught up in my own excitement I didn't notice I was moving too fast for my congregation. What seemed enlightening and transformative to me was, for many in my congregation, confusing and even unsettling. I had unintentionally created a gap between us, and the bond we once shared began to weaken. The congregation I loved and had walked with for years began to feel lost, disconnected from the teachings they once found familiar and comforting.

When I finally realized what was happening, it was a sobering moment. I could see my eagerness had caused me to lose sight of my primary role as a pastor—to guide, support, and nurture my congregation. I had become so focused on introducing new theological concepts that I had forgotten to consider the pace at which my people could comfortably walk with me on this journey. The responsibility I felt as their leader weighed heavily on me.

So, I did the only thing I could do: I apologized. I stood before my congregation and said, "I love you. We have walked through this life journey together, and I don't want to lose you. So, tell me, where did I lose you?" This apology wasn't just about admitting I had moved too quickly; it was about reaffirming my commitment to them, to our shared journey, and to ensuring no one felt left behind. It was a plea for their understanding and a desire to find our way back to each other.

In that moment, I rediscovered my pastor's heart. I admitted in my joyful passion for theological exploration, I had made a mistake. I asked for another chance to reconnect, to slow down, and to start over if necessary. I returned to the Bible for a season, not because I had abandoned my broader understanding of God, but because I wanted to reassure my congregation, to meet them where they were, and bring them along at a pace they could handle.

This experience taught me the power of apology. It is more than just a way to mend relationships; it is a crucial part of leadership. It reinforced for me the importance of humility in leadership. It reminded me that while the pursuit of knowledge and understanding is important, it must never come at the expense of the people you are called to serve. The power of an apology lies in its ability to heal, to restore, and to strengthen the bonds holding us together.

YOUR *LifeWork*

Message: As a minister or a layperson, recognize when you've moved too quickly or lost touch with your community. Tap into the power of a sincere apology in restoring connection and trust. Emphasize true leadership involves not just sharing new ideas but also listening, admitting mistakes, and ensuring everyone feels included on the journey.

Implementation:

- *Model and Promote the Apology Process*: In a sermon or discussion, share a personal story where you've realized you moved too fast or lost touch with your congregation, and explain how you made amends. This sets an example of humility and the importance of making things right. Develop a lesson or workshop on the importance of apologies in leadership. Highlight how apologies can bridge gaps and restore trust within a community. Encourage members of your community to practice apologies in their own lives when they recognize they have moved too fast or made mistakes, whether in personal relationships or in leadership roles.

- *Check Your Faith Community's Pulse*: Establish regular check-ins with your congregation where they can provide feedback on recent teachings or changes. Make it clear this feedback is valued and will be acted upon if necessary. Create a safe space in your church or community where members can share if and when they feel overwhelmed or disconnected by new teachings. Use this as an opportunity to listen and learn where you may need to slow down or clarify your messages.

- *Revisit Foundational Teachings*: If you've introduced new and complex ideas recently, take some time to revisit more familiar teachings. This helps to reassure and reconnect with those who may have felt left behind.

- *Practice Patience in Teaching*: Be mindful of the pace at which you introduce new concepts. Break down complex ideas into smaller, more digestible parts and check in with your audience to ensure they are following along.

Reflection Exercise: As a minister or a layperson, ask yourself these questions: *Have I introduced new ideas too quickly without considering if my faith community is ready for them? When was the last time I asked for feedback from those I lead? How did I respond to that feedback? Have I ever apologized to my faith community? How was it received? How do I know when my congregation or group is feeling overwhelmed or disconnected? Do I have systems in place to gauge this? What steps can I take to ensure I am leading at a pace everyone can follow?* Then consider when it makes sense to ask members these same questions.

Affirmation: "I am certain that certainty is uncertain. I will be flexible, malleable, versatile, agile, and mobile as I celebrate the certainty of uncertainty."

— D.E. Paulk and LaDonna Paulk Diaz
from *Fully Awake 365* (2022)

SMALL WINS MATTER:
CELEBRATE BABY STEPS

I've always believed in the power of small wins. The incremental steps might seem insignificant in the grand scheme of things; but they are actually the foundation upon which greater change is built. This idea was brought home to me in a powerful way when I heard about a well-known minister in my community. He had recently baptized the child of a same-gender loving couple—a small act with potentially enormous implications.

When this minister faced criticism from conservative members and fellow clergy, his response was, "Why should the child suffer for the parents' sin?" As someone who deeply values inclusion, this response was jarring and offensive. The idea of labeling the love between two people as sin is ignorant and deeply harmful. However, I couldn't help but see a sliver of progress in his words. Many ministers in my area at that time wouldn't even consider offering this sacrament to such a couple under any circumstances. This slight shift, this tiny crack in the wall of prejudice, is what I've come to recognize as a "cloud the size of a man's hand" (The Holy Bible, New King James Version, 1 Kings 18:44). It's small, almost imperceptible, but it's a sign change is coming, that the sound of an abundance of rain is beginning to echo in our hearts.

I think about Bishop Pearson, who started his Inclusion Journey from a place of deep-rooted bias. Early on, he would say things like, "You can BE gay, and not DO gay," a statement is undeniably offensive. Yet, at that time, it represented a huge leap forward for him. For a holiness preacher like Bishop Pearson, acknowledging it was okay to be gay—even if he didn't yet fully understand or accept the LGBTQ+ community—was a massive step. Years later, he would become a passionate advocate for marriage equality, performing countless same-gender weddings. But, what if those around him had written him off during his early, more awkward attempts at understanding? What if they had been too offended to see the progress he was making?

Looking back, I see the importance of patience and the power of small wins. It's easy to be offended by the ignorance often accompanying early attempts at inclusion. I've learned that staying the course, offering grace, and recognizing even the smallest steps forward can contribute to a person's journey toward a more inclusive mindset. Those small victories, however imperfect, are crucial—they're the seeds that eventually grow into a more inclusive faith community. Celebrating them isn't about ignoring the harm they may still carry; it's about recognizing the potential for growth and change, and understanding every step forward, no matter how small, is worth acknowledging. Those baby steps, no matter how frustrating they may seem, are the very steps leading to greater understanding and acceptance.

YOUR *LifeWork*

Message: As a minister or a layperson, recognize and celebrate the small victories on your Inclusion Journey, even when those victories are imperfect or come with elements that might still offend. By acknowledging these baby steps, we encourage further growth and foster a more inclusive environment within our communities.

Implementation:

- *Acknowledge Progress Publicly*: In your sermons, talks, or group discussions, highlight instances where individuals or institutions have taken steps toward inclusion, no matter how small. Set up a space in your community where people can post and share small victories related to inclusion. This could be as simple as a member attending their first Pride event or a local business deciding to use more inclusive language in their communications.
- *Support Those on Their Journey*: Commit to mentoring or supporting someone who is in the early stages of understanding or embracing inclusion. Encourage them, even if their language or actions are not yet fully aligned with inclusive ideals. Conduct a

workshop or discussion series on the importance of incremental change in social justice movements. Explain how small actions, over time, contribute to significant shifts in societal attitudes and behaviors.

- *Promote Forgiveness and Patience*: Teach about the importance of patience and forgiveness as others grow in their understanding of inclusion. Share stories from religious texts or personal experiences emphasizing the value of supporting others, even when they make mistakes.
- *Encourage Conscious Language*: Host a session on how to gradually adopt more inclusive language within your community. Offer practical tips on how to address others respectfully and how to correct language that may be unintentionally harmful.
- *Celebrate Together*: Organize events or services specifically dedicated to celebrating small steps toward inclusion within your community. Use these moments to reflect on the progress made and to inspire continued efforts.

Reflection Exercise: As a minister or a layperson, ask yourself these questions: *Have I recently encountered someone making an effort toward inclusion that felt imperfect or offensive? How did I respond? Am I able to recognize and celebrate small steps toward inclusion, even when they fall short of my ideals? How can I better support individuals in my community who are in the early stages of embracing inclusion? What biases or cultural conditioning might I still hold preventing me from fully supporting incremental progress? How can I model patience and forgiveness when others are trying to grow in their understanding of inclusion?* Then consider when it makes sense to ask members these same questions.

THINK SPACE: The choice is yours! Take notes, draw, doodle, and

Prayer: "Re-Creating Spirit, reshape, clear out and carve away anything that keeps me from my highest and greatest good. Amen.

— D.E. Paulk and LaDonna Paulk Diaz
from *Fully Awake 365* (2022)

DITCH UNIFORMITY,
EMBRACE DIVERSITY

Every Sunday, as I look out at the faces in my congregation, I'm struck by the vast array of beliefs and experiences defining us. The concepts of the devil, hell, and salvation are often points of contention, and for many, they can be deal breakers. But rather than getting bogged down in these theological debates, I've chosen to avoid making deals altogether—especially not with the devil. My mission is to cultivate a spiritual community that respects each person's agency and embraces our collective diversity.

The ultimate goal isn't to create a church that is uniform in its theology or politics. Every person in the pews before me is an individual, carrying their unique set of beliefs, experiences, and worldviews. And so, inclusion must reflect this reality.

Inclusion often carries a liberal tone, particularly within the western context. LGBTQ+ affirmation, for instance, is a significant aspect of inclusion and tends to lean left. Similarly, approaching the Bible through a historical-critical methodology is more common in liberal seminaries than in conservative Bible schools. These observations are not just anecdotal; they are quantitatively measurable and justifiable. As I continue to guide my congregation along this Inclusion Journey, I remain mindful every member carries complex political views.

Inclusion speaks for itself. There is no need to politicize this message in a way that creates division within our congregation. Jesus, after all, condemned wealth but also promoted wise financial investment. Paul, too, held a mix of values, blending Socialist principles with Conservative ideals. The transition to inclusion does not demand we all think the same way politically. Though my church is predominantly African-American, the diversity of political and religious beliefs is vast. Some members are veterans or active military, while others have dedicated their lives to social justice, working closely with leaders like Rev. Jesse Jackson, Dr. Coretta Scott King, and Rev. Al Sharpton. I've walked alongside *Black Lives Matter* activists and served as a police chaplain, embodying the complexity which defines our community. We are as complex as we are typical.

Our life experiences shape how we see the world and how we understand God. As I preach and teach, I'm aware each person hears my words through their own set of filters, colored by their memories and experiences. Inclusion, therefore, does not require us to think or believe in exactly the same way. As Bishop Carlton Pearson wisely said, "We can mind the same things without always having the same mind." This sentiment guides me as I lead our congregation into a future where inclusion is not just acknowledged but embraced.

YOUR *LifeWork*

Message: As a minister or a layperson, understand fostering an inclusive community doesn't mean everyone must think alike. Embrace and celebrate the diverse beliefs, political views, and life experiences within your congregation. Your role is to create a spiritual environment where every individual feels respected and valued, regardless of their theological or political stance.

Implementation:

- *Conduct Crucial Conversations*: Host regular discussions or small group sessions where members can openly share their diverse viewpoints on theological topics, such as the concepts of hell, salvation, or social justice, without fear of judgment. Promote a culture of respect when discussing political issues. Encourage members to listen to one another's political perspectives, reminding them inclusion is about mutual respect, not uniformity.
- *Embrace Diverse Worship Practices*: Incorporate various worship styles and traditions into your services reflecting the cultural and theological diversity of your congregation. This might include

different musical genres, prayers, or liturgies from various faith traditions.

- *Celebrate Individual Stories*: Create opportunities for members to share their personal faith journeys and how their life experiences have shaped their views of God and spirituality. This could be through testimonies, blog posts, or video stories shared with the congregation.
- *Support Diverse Ministries*: Engage in and support ministries serving various aspects of your community's diversity—whether racial, socio-economic, or political diversity. Highlight the importance of these ministries in your communications.

Reflection Exercise: As a minister or a layperson, ask yourself these questions: *How do my personal beliefs and experiences shape my approach to inclusion? How am I actively creating space for diverse voices and perspectives within my spiritual community? What steps am I taking to ensure our community respects political and theological differences? How can I model civil discourse and mutual respect when discussing sensitive topics like politics or theology? What biases do I need to address within myself to foster a truly inclusive environment?* Then consider when it makes sense to ask members these same questions.

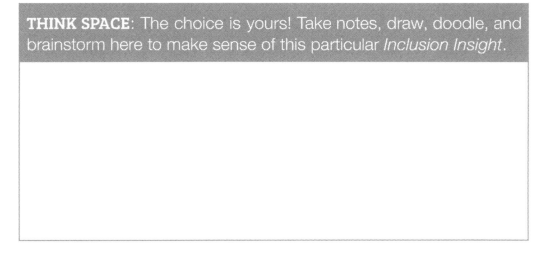

THINK SPACE: The choice is yours! Take notes, draw, doodle, and brainstorm here to make sense of this particular *Inclusion Insight*.

Affirmation: "I am willing to say, 'I don't know' - and that's beautiful."

— D.E. Paulk and LaDonna Paulk Diaz
from *Fully Awake 365* (2022)

FINANCE, FRUGALITY, FREEDOM

When I first began this journey into inclusion, I never imagined how closely my financial habits would intertwine with my theological integrity. The pulpit, a place where truth is meant to be spoken without hesitation, began to feel like a stage where my own insecurities about money dictated my performance. Financial stewardship, I realized, was not just about managing money—it was about managing the freedom to speak my truth, unhindered by the weight of financial instability.

For years, I navigated life paycheck to paycheck, always feeling that gnawing insecurity, the fear of one wrong move, one sermon too radical, might result in the loss of financial support. It was as if my bank account and my beliefs were in a constant tug-of-war, each pulling me in different directions. But this struggle also taught me something valuable. Living hand-to-mouth, as frustrating and limiting as it was, also served as an unlikely teacher. It forced me to pause, to think carefully before introducing new and potentially controversial ideas. In a way, it kept me grounded, ensuring I did not rush headlong into changes I—or my congregation—were not ready for.

I knew if I desired to truly live out the principles of inclusion, I would need to find a way to divorce my financial fears from my theological convictions. The first step was to take a hard look at my spending habits. *Gospel Hollywood*, with its glamorous facade, had set a standard both unrealistic and unsustainable for someone in my position. The fancy cars, the designer clothes, the lavish vacations—they were all distractions, pulling me away from the simplicity and sincerity that inclusion required.

I decided to recalibrate my budget, not as an act of deprivation, but as an act of empowerment. I stripped away the unnecessary luxuries and focused on what truly mattered—security and peace of mind. Transitioning into inclusion might not be the most lucrative path, but it was one that offered a different kind of wealth. A wealth rooted in authenticity, in the joy coming from being true to oneself.

As I continue to build this new theological house, I am acutely aware of the costs. Overspending and living on the financial edge can no longer be part of my reality. The thrill of shopping sprees and the temporary high of new possessions pale in comparison to the deep, lasting joy of living in alignment with my values. Financial freedom, I've learned, is not just about having enough money—it's about ensuring money, or the lack of it, never dictates the truth I choose to speak. It allows me to stand in the pulpit and preach with a clear conscience, knowing that my truth is not for sale.

YOUR *LifeWork*

Message: As a minister or a layperson, teach the profound connection between financial stewardship and the freedom to live and speak your truth. The way you manage your finances can either empower you to preach and live authentically or bind you with fear and hesitation. To fully embrace the principles of inclusion, it is essential to create a life where financial security supports rather than hinders your spiritual and theological journey.

Implementation:

- *Create a Personal Budget*: Take time to develop a realistic budget aligned with your current financial situation and future goals. Ensure it prioritizes financial security over luxury, focusing on needs rather than wants. Identify areas where you are "spending" money to keep up with appearances or out of habit rather than necessity. Begin cutting back on these expenses to free up resources for more meaningful pursuits.
- *Teach Financial Stewardship*: As a minister or layperson, consider holding workshops or classes on financial management within your community. Equip others with the tools to budget effectively, avoid debt, and live within their means. Consider redefining and

reframing "spending" as "circulating" and root this in the concepts of giving and receiving.

- *Support Others in Financial Struggles*: Be a source of support and guidance for those in your community who may be struggling financially. Offer advice, resources, or simply a listening ear to help them navigate their challenges.
- *Model Simplicity*: Lead by example by adopting a lifestyle prioritizing simplicity and authenticity over materialism. Share your journey with others, demonstrating true joy and freedom come from living in alignment with your values. Regularly evaluate your material possessions and money circulation habits. Ask yourself if they truly serve your purpose or if they are distractions from your spiritual and personal growth.

Reflection Exercise: As a minister or a layperson, ask yourself these questions: *How does my current financial situation affect my ability to speak and live my truth? What fears do I have about money, and how do they influence my decisions in life and ministry? How can I simplify my life to focus more on what truly matters, rather than on accumulating material possessions? What steps can I take to gain financial security and freedom in support of my spiritual journey? How can I create a more supportive community addressing the intersection of financial and spiritual well-being?* Then consider when it makes sense to ask members these same questions.

THINK SPACE: The choice is yours! Take notes, draw, doodle, and brainstorm here to make sense of this particular *Inclusion Insight*.

Prayer: "Christ Consciousness, help me to understand that there is no separation between me and God. Amen."

— D.E. Paulk and LaDonna Paulk Diaz
from *Fully Awake 365* (2022)

PRAY THEN MOVE YOUR FEET

I used to believe faith was primarily about Orthodoxy—having the "right belief," the correct understanding of doctrine and theology. But over time, I began to see this focus on belief alone was insufficient for the kind of spiritual transformation I was seeking. The more I delved into the teachings of various faith traditions, the more I realized Orthopraxy, the "right action," was equally, if not more, important.

There was a time when I found myself stuck in a theological rut. I was surrounded by beliefs passed down for generations, and any attempt to question or shift these beliefs was met with resistance. But then, I encountered a group of people who lived out their faith in a way new to me—same-gender loving individuals who radiated love, Hindus who embodied compassion, and atheists who were altruistic in their actions. The conversations, the shared meals, and the simple acts of kindness made me realize theology could indeed be recast through exposure to the compassionate lives of others. These encounters began to reshape my understanding of what it meant to live out my faith.

One of the key moments in this journey was when I came across the Jewish saying, "the heart follows the deeds." This simple truth resonated deeply with me. It suggested if I wanted to experience a shift in my beliefs, I needed to start with action. It wasn't about forcing a change in theology but about engaging in acts of kindness and service naturally leading to a broader, more inclusive understanding of faith.

The words of James, "faith without works is dead," took on new meaning for me. I had always understood faith to be a matter of the heart and mind, but now I saw it was also a matter of the hands and feet. It was in the doing that my faith came alive. And, as I began to focus more on Orthopraxy, I noticed the barriers between different faiths and ways of life started to dissolve.

Siddhartha Gautama's concept of the "Middle Way" also influenced my thinking. He believed right thinking, right action, and right livelihood should be in harmony, creating a balance and leading to a meaningful and ethical life. This idea of balance became a cornerstone of my spiritual practice. I realized I could no longer separate belief from action; they needed to inform and support each other. With this new understanding, I became more intentional about my involvement in community service and social justice work. I sought out opportunities to engage with people who challenged my perspectives, whether it was through volunteering at a shelter for those experiencing homelessness, organizing interfaith events, or simply listening to the stories of those who were different from me. These experiences not only broadened my understanding of the world, they also deepened my faith in ways I had not anticipated.

I came to see the divisions between evangelism and the social gospel as artificial. Both were essential aspects of living out my faith. By embracing Orthopraxy, I found my theology began to evolve naturally, shaped by the relationships and experiences engaging with the world around me.

In the end, I learned prayer must be followed by action. It is not enough to pray for change; we must also move our feet and be the change we seek. This is the essence of Orthopraxic transformation—a faith alive, dynamic, and rooted in the reality of lived experience. Through this journey, I discovered true spiritual growth comes not from clinging to old beliefs but from stepping out in faith and letting our actions lead the way.

YOUR *LifeWork*

Message: As a minister or a layperson, recognize faith is not just about what you believe, but how you live out those beliefs through action. Lean into Orthopraxy, where your deeds and service to others naturally reshape and deepen your understanding of faith. Engage in activities which bring you into contact with diverse groups of people, and let your actions be the catalyst for both personal and communal transformation.

Implementation:

- *Encourage Personal Acts of Service*: Challenge your congregation or small group to commit to one act of service in direct contact with someone different from themselves each week. Share these experiences in group settings to inspire and learn from each other.
- *Teach on the Middle Way*: Introduce the concept of the Middle Way from Buddhism in a teaching or workshop. Discuss how right thinking, right action, and right livelihood intersect with Christian principles and how these can be applied in daily life.
- *Develop a "Faith in Action" Journal*: Encourage members to keep a journal where they record their acts of service, the people they meet, and the reflections on how these experiences are impacting their faith. Share insights from these journals in a communal setting.
- *Plan an Interfaith Community Outreach Event*: Collaborate with leaders from other faith communities to create a joint service project. Organize an event involving partnering with diverse groups. Ensure participants include individuals from various backgrounds and beliefs. This could be a cleanup campaign, a food drive, or another charitable activity bringing people together across religious lines.

Reflection Exercise: As a minister or a layperson, ask yourself these questions: *How often do I engage in actions directly reflecting my faith? In what ways have my beliefs been shaped or reshaped by my interactions with those who hold different views? Do I prioritize Orthodoxy (right belief) over Orthopraxy (right action) in my spiritual life? Why or why not? What steps can I take to ensure my faith is lived out in practical, compassionate ways in my community? How can I create opportunities for myself and others to practice faith through service and promote greater understanding and compassion?* Then consider when it makes sense to ask members these same questions.

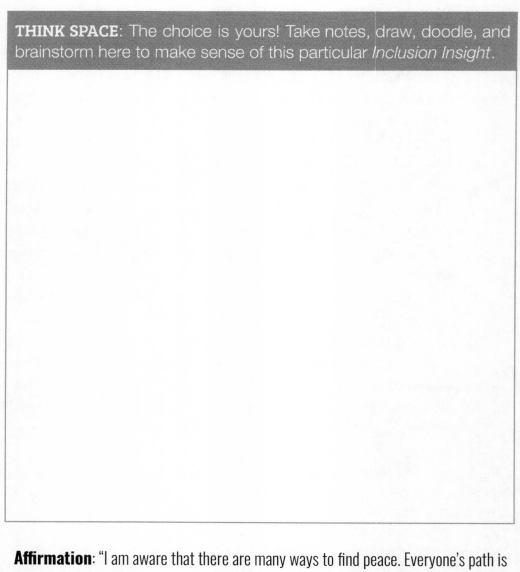

Affirmation: "I am aware that there are many ways to find peace. Everyone's path is different and no two journeys are exactly the same. I will not spend my life arguing with others about their chosen path. Instead, I will ask myself the only question that really matters: Is It Working For Me?"

— D.E. Paulk and LaDonna Paulk Diaz
from *Fully Awake 365* (2022)

GO TO HELL (OR NOT)!

When I first encountered the concept of inclusion in theology, it seemed almost too good to be true—a God who would not let a single soul be lost to hell, and a Jesus who accomplished complete reconciliation for all humanity. This vision of divine love was all-encompassing, offering grace even to the most wayward of souls. However, as a biblical scholar, historically critical theologian, and Civil and Human Rights activist, my journey to embrace theodicy (attempting to reconcile a good God with human suffering and the moral evils in the world) has been complex. As I delved deeper into this idea, I was confronted with some disturbing questions: *What about those who have committed horrendous crimes, like Hitler? Can such individuals really end up in the same heaven as saints like Mother Teresa?*

The thought of entirely abolishing hell was not just challenging; it felt irresponsible. For those who have suffered under the hands of oppressors or who have been deeply wronged, how could I reconcile a God of justice with what might seem like a careless, blanket forgiveness? It felt as though, in striving for inclusion, I might be sacrificing the very essence of moral accountability.

And yet, I began to see that perhaps the issue wasn't with the concept of hell itself, but with how I had been defining it. Rather than seeing hell as a place of eternal torment, I started to consider it as a process of purging—a temporary, refining fire that could cleanse rather than destroy. In this view, hell is not the antithesis of heaven, but a necessary step for some souls to undergo a transformation to align them with divine love.

This perspective helped me embrace a God who does not ignore or trivialize evil but who addresses it with the same love that seeks to include all in the Divine family. It's a love that is strong enough to hold space for justice, without resorting to eternal damnation. Hell, redefined in this way, becomes a part of the journey toward wholeness and unity, where even those who have done the most harm are not beyond the reach of divine grace, but are instead given the opportunity for redemption and renewal.

Inclusion, then, is not about erasing consequences or dismissing the need for justice. It is about trusting in a God who is both just and merciful, who can hold the tension between grace and accountability, and who ultimately desires to restore all of creation, even if that means going through hell to get there.

YOUR LifeWork

Message: As a minister or a layperson, rethink and redefine your view of hell to communicate a more nuanced understanding of divine justice and mercy. Embrace a vision of God's love that includes accountability without resorting to eternal condemnation, while still addressing the need for justice in the face of profound evil. Teach that God's love is not about ignoring or excusing wrongdoing but about transforming and restoring all of creation.

Implementation:

- *Teach a Series on Divine Justice and Mercy*: Develop a small group study series to explore the themes of divine justice, mercy, and the possibility of rethinking hell as a purifying process rather than eternal punishment. Use biblical examples to illustrate how God's love can coexist with justice.

- *Discussion Thorny Theological Questions*: Organize a discussion group where participants can wrestle with challenging theological concepts like the nature of hell, the fate of those who commit atrocities, and how these ideas intersect with God's love and justice. Encourage open and respectful dialogue.

- *Preach on the Transformative Power of Divine Love*: Teach about the transformative power of God's love, explaining how this love can purify and restore even those who have committed great wrongs. Encourage your congregation to see divine justice as a process of healing rather than mere retribution.

- *Offer Workshops on Forgiveness and Accountability*: Facilitate workshops to help members understand how to balance forgiveness with accountability in their personal lives, reflecting the Divine model of justice and mercy. Consider resources such as, *Radical Forgiveness: A Revolutionary Five-Stage Process to: Heal Relationships, Let Go of Anger and Blame, and Find Peace in Any Situation* (Tipping, 2002).

Reflection Exercise: As a minister or a layperson, ask yourself these questions: *How do I currently understand the concept of hell, and how has this understanding influenced my view of God's justice and mercy? What are the implications of redefining hell in a way that aligns with both justice and inclusion? How can I communicate the idea of a purifying, restorative hell without diminishing the seriousness of sin and injustice? In what ways might this new understanding of hell change how I approach pastoral care, especially for those who have suffered deep wounds? How do I reconcile the idea of divine justice with the notion of God's all-encompassing love?* Then consider when it makes sense to ask members these same questions.

THINK SPACE: The choice is yours! Take notes, draw, doodle, and brainstorm here to make sense of this particular *Inclusion Insight*.

Prayer: "Mother God, help me to remember that we are all feminine as well as masculine and that one without the other is incomplete. Help me to embrace all of myself today and to honor all of my characteristics equally. Amen."

— D.E. Paulk and LaDonna Paulk Diaz
from *Fully Awake 365* (2022)

ORDERED STEPS:
CHILDREN GO WHERE WE SEND THEE

Over the years, one of the most common concerns I've heard from parents and guardians of children and teens is, "My children need a solid biblical foundation." This statement, while sincere, reflects an underlying anxiety about the kind of world their children will face as they grow. By giving their children a strong grounding in scripture, they hope their children will be better prepared to navigate life's challenges and make sound moral choices. As a biblical scholar, I often feel conflicted about this sentiment. Yes, the Bible is foundational, but it's also true much of what we teach from it can be harmful if approached without care. Parents and guardians want their children to grow up with spiritual roots, but I believe there is a better way to engage them with the Bible to foster a deep, personal connection to divine wisdom without burdening them with dogma.

In many churches, there is a theological imbalance between the way we engage adults and children. Adults are often given more room to explore their faith, to question and reinterpret scripture based on their experiences and insights. Children, on the other hand, are frequently given a simplified version of faith, one emphasizing obedience and moral lessons over personal exploration and spiritual growth. This can unintentionally stifle the spiritual development of young people, preventing them from forming their own relationship with the Divine. To truly foster inclusion, we must work towards theological harmony across all areas of ministry, especially when it comes to children and youth. Their spiritual curriculum needs rethinking. We need to find ways to teach biblical principles without simply molding our children into little missionaries who parrot doctrines they may not fully understand. Instead, let's guide them in exploring the Bible with open minds and hearts, letting them see the beauty and wisdom within without turning them into soldiers of a rigid faith.

This slow, deliberate shift in theology—away from fear-based spirituality towards one rooted in love and inner wisdom—is essential for the future of our ministry. Fear-based faith, while effective in controlling behavior, often leaves little room for grace or personal transformation. It can create a culture of anxiety, where children are taught to be more concerned with following the rules than cultivating a genuine relationship with God. Indeed, a faith rooted in love allows for mistakes, growth, and deeper understanding. It fosters a sense of belonging and inclusion, where everyone is invited to experience the Divine in their own unique way.

By taking the time to thoughtfully reconsider how we engage children with scripture, we can help them develop a faith that is both strong and flexible, capable of withstanding the inevitable challenges they will face in life. It's a transition that won't happen overnight, but it will open the door for a deeper, more inclusive experience of faith for everyone, especially our children. This is not about abandoning tradition but about expanding it, making room for a new generation to encounter the sacred in ways that speak to their hearts and minds. In doing so, we prepare them not just to follow in our footsteps but to walk their own path with confidence, wisdom, and love.

YOUR *LifeWork*

Message: As a minister or a layperson, one of your most vital roles is to ensure theological harmony exists within your faith community, especially when it comes to the spiritual formation of children and youth. It's essential to move beyond doctrinal rigidity and fear-based teaching, guiding the congregation—especially the younger members—toward a deeper understanding of the Bible that emphasizes love, wisdom, and divine connection.

Implementation:

- *Rethink Curriculum Design*: Review the current children's and youth curriculum to ensure it promotes exploration of biblical teachings rather than strict doctrinal adherence. Incorporate more lessons on love, wisdom, and divine connection.

- *Host Inclusive Bible Study Sessions*: Organize Bible study groups for youth to encourage questions and open dialogue, emphasizing that the Bible is a source of wisdom and guidance rather than *the* sole source of wisdom or a rulebook.

- *Collaborate with Families*: Engage parents and guardians in discussions about the spiritual development of their children. Reassure them that a more inclusive, love-based approach to biblical teachings will provide a strong, compassionate foundation for their children.

- *Facilitate Youth-Led Discussions*: Allow youth to lead conversations about their understanding of biblical stories and how these lessons can be applied in ways that promote inclusion and spiritual maturity.

- *Wean from Fear-Based Theology*: Slowly guide the congregation away from fear-driven narratives by preaching and teaching more about the love and wisdom that exists within, helping them reframe how they view their relationship with the Divine.

Reflection Exercise: As a minister or a layperson, ask yourself these questions: *How does the current children's and youth curriculum reflect the inclusion and wisdom we want to promote within the church? Am I encouraging young people to explore the Bible with an open heart, or am I pushing them toward a specific doctrine or set of beliefs? How can I help parents and guardians feel comfortable with a more open, love-based approach to spiritual teaching for their children? Have I created spaces where youth feel free to express their spiritual ideas without fear of judgment or correction?* Then consider when it makes sense to ask members these same questions.

Affirmation: "The Universe will send to me whatever I need for the evolution of my consciousness. I am open and available for this growth and unfoldment...however it finds its way to me."

— D.E. Paulk and LaDonna Paulk Diaz
from *Fully Awake 365* (2022)

YOUR INCLUSION INSIGHTS

Although you've come to the end of this workbook, it is not the end of your Inclusion Journey. Along the way, as you've read this workbook, you've likely uncovered an *Inclusion Insight* (or perhaps more) that resonates deeply with your experience. The following space is designed for you to capture those thoughts, insights, and ideas as they emerge and distill them into your own *Inclusion Insights*. Once you've written your *Inclusion Insight*, take a moment to reflect using the following questions:

- What does your insight mean to you personally or in your ministry?
- How can you apply your insight to your daily life or interactions within your faith community?
- What challenges might you face in implementing your insight, and how can you address them?

After reflecting on what you've written, I encourage you to share your *Inclusion Insight* with others in your faith community. These shared reflections help foster collective growth and inspire deeper understanding within the group. I'd love to see your *Inclusion Insight* as well! Feel free to email your writings to me at pastor@mytruthsanctuary.com. Your Inclusion Journey continues, and I'm excited to witness how you contribute to building more inclusive and compassionate communities. Happy writing and reflecting!

[ADD YOUR INSIGHT TITLE HERE]

Introduction: Introduce your *Inclusion Insight* idea. You could even tell a story!

_____
_____
_____
_____
_____
_____
_____
_____

Definition and Explanation: Define the main points of your *Inclusion Insight* idea.

_____
_____
_____
_____
_____
_____
_____
_____
_____

Why It Matters: Explain why your *Inclusion Insight* is important by highlighting spiritual and practical benefits.

_____
_____
_____
_____
_____
_____
_____
_____

Scriptural or Theological Reflection: Share a relevant scripture or theological concept to support your *Inclusion Insight*.   Briefly tell how this scripture or theological concept ties into your *Inclusion Insight.*

_____

_____

_____

_____

_____

_____

_____

_____

_____

Practical Application: Share 2 to 3 practical steps or exercises to be done for your *Inclusion Insight.*

_____

_____

_____

_____

_____

_____

_____

_____

_____

Prayer: "Spirit of Rebirth, thank You for placing eternity in my heart. I am reborn every moment that I realize my journey is one of spiritual growth and eternal expansion. Amen."

— D.E. Paulk and LaDonna Paulk Diaz
from *Fully Awake 365* (2022)

REFERENCES

Ammerman, Nancy, Carl Dudley, Jackson Carroll, and William McKinney. *Studying Congregations: A New Handbook*. Abingdon Press, 1998, p. 123.

Bridges, William. *Managing Transitions: Making the Most of Change*. 4th ed., Da Capo Press, 2016.

Buddha. *The Dhammapada*. Translated by Thomas Byrom, Shambhala, 1993.

Crouch, Orlando, and Gary Oliver. *Welcome Into This Place*. Triumph Worship, 1987.

Dalai Lama. *The Art of Happiness: A Handbook for Living*. Riverhead, 1998.

Doniger, Wendy. *The Implied Spider: Politics and Theology in Myth*. Columbia University Press, 1998.

Elkins, David N. Beyond Religion: A Personal Program for Building a Spiritual Life Outside the Walls of Traditional Religion. Quest Books, 1998.

Fox, Emmet. *The Sermon on the Mount: The Key to Success in Life*. Harper & Brothers, 1938.

Geddes, Patrick. *Cities in Evolution*. Williams & Norgate, 1915.

Johnson, Benton. "Sociological Theory and Religious Truth." *Sociological Analysis*, vol. 38, no. 4, 1977.

Jones, Mitchell L., and Tony Lamair Burks II. *The Journey to Authenticity: 8 Secrets to Getting the Life You Desire*. L3 Publishing LLC, 2016.

Paulk, D.E., and LaDonna Paulk Diaz. *Fully Awake 365: Challenge Your Mind, Channel Your Power, and Change Your Life*. Spirit and Truth Sanctuary, 2022.

Pearson, Carlton D. *The Gospel of Inclusion: Reaching Beyond Religious Fundamentalism to the True Love of God and Self.* Atria Books, 2006.

Roberts, Kara. "Towards a New Comparative Methodology in Religious Studies." *JSTOR*, 2018, www.jstor.org.

Tipping, Colin. *Radical Forgiveness: A Revolutionary Five-Stage Process to Heal Relationships, Let Go of Anger and Blame, and Find Peace in Any Situation.* Sounds True, 2002.

Womack, Deanna Ferree. *Neighbors: Christians and Muslims Building Community.* Westminster John Knox Press, 2020, pp. 122-123.

The Holy Bible. New King James Version, Thomas Nelson, 1982.

ABOUT THE AUTHORS

BISHOP D.E. PAULK is the Senior Pastor of *Spirit & Truth Sanctuary*, located in metropolitan Atlanta (Decatur, Georgia), where he successfully transitioned an Evangelical Charismatic church into a thriving interfaith, LGBTQ+ affirming spiritual collective. He is also the co-founder and presiding prelate of the *International Communion of Expanding Consciousness* (I.C.E.C.), an ecumenical network offering covering, fellowship, and ministry credentials to those desirous of creating and sustaining inclusive spiritual communities.

As successor of the late Bishop Carlton D. Pearson, he is a board member of the Carlton D. Pearson Legacy Foundation, host of the weekly broadcast *Bishop Carlton D. Pearson's: The Gospel of Inclusion* and is committed to carrying on the mission, communicating the message, and continuing the mandate of Inclusion.

Bishop Paulk holds a Master of Theological Studies (M.T.S., Global Religions) from Emory University's Candler School of Theology and is currently pursuing a Doctorate of Ministry (D.Min.) in Scriptural Interpretation. He travels internationally to equip pastors and laity with an effective methodological approach to architecting Inclusion with sensitivities to church culture, scriptural context, and concerns for financial solvency.

In 2008, Bishop Paulk was inducted into the Morehouse College Dr. Martin Luther King, Jr. International Board of Preachers. In 2010, he was asked to serve as a National Board Member for the Southern Christian Leadership Conference (SCLC), the historic civil rights organization founded by Dr. Martin Luther King, Jr. His family founded *The Cathedral of the Holy Spirit* (formerly *Chapel Hill Harvester Church*) in 1960. By the Fall of 1961, and in the legacy of Dr. Howard Washington Thurman, Dr. Alfred Fisk, and *The Church for the Fellowship of All Peoples*, the Paulk Family curated the southeast's first racially integrated church.

Bishop Paulk is the founder of the Pro-Love organization, a social justice collective purposed to deconstruct social and religious hierarchies and designed to promote racial equity, marriage equality, and interfaith education. He is widely known as a radically inclusive minister who perceives Spirit to be evenly present in all of creation and discoverable via diverse paths and disparate philosophies.

Bishop Paulk has authored several books including *I Don't Know...The Way of Knowing* (an invitation into the esoteric celebration of Beginner's Mind); *The Holy Bible of Inclusion* (an in-depth exegetical, anti-apologetic work defending doctrines of Universal Salvation and ecclesiastical, ecumenical expressions of Inclusivity); and *Fully Awake 365* (a yearlong daily devotional reaching into the higher recesses of self-actualization and realms of innate, inner, and inherent divinity).

Bishop Paulk makes his home in suburban Atlanta along with his wife, Brandi, and children, Esther and Micah.

❖

A seeker and a connector, DR. TONY LAMAIR BURKS II first learned about New Thought from his paternal grandmother, an avid reader of *Daily Word*. He was raised in both the African Methodist Episcopal Church and Missionary Baptist Church, and experienced a broad landscape of spirituality as an undergraduate. He attended the Martin Luther King Jr. International Chapel, the Shrine of the Black Madonna, Butler Street Baptist Church, and Hillside International Truth Center.

After college, he joined nondenominational churches and United Methodist churches before becoming a member of Saint James Presbyterian Church. His diverse church membership, studies at the Barbara King School of Ministry (BKSM), and the collective ministerial legacy of his grandfather, Rev. Timothy M. Burks, and great great grandfather, "Preachin'" John Grubbs, inform his approach to pastoral care.

He is a torchbearer and is among the last cohort of 12 students to learn at the feet of world spiritual leader, Bishop Dr. Barbara Lewis King.

A member of *The Society of Professional Obituary Writers*, he has written obituaries for over a third of a century in ways that honor loved ones. He is an award-winning educator who has served schools, districts, and nonprofits in roles from teacher and principal to director and area superintendent.

As a writer, he has contributed to national and international projects including the anthology, *The Leader Reader: Narratives of Experience*, and the "When They See Us", "Colin in Black & White", "Queen Sugar" and "Origin" learning companions for filmmaker Ava DuVernay. A two-time graduate of BKSM, he is an ordained minister and a graduate of Morehouse College, Trevecca Nazarene University, and the University of North Carolina at Greensboro. He has lived in Atlanta's historic Washington Park neighborhood since 2012. The father of an adult son, he and his beloved are the parents of a little girl.

ENGAGING THE AUTHORS

Bishop Paulk is available for
Speaking Engagements and Seminary Lectures
"A Day of Seminary" Training for Ministers and Laity
Ministerial Covering, Credentialing, and Ordination
Inclusive Church Planting and more!

bishop@mytruthsanctuary.com
mytruthsanctuary.com
mytruthsanctuary.com/products
myicec.com
404-243-5020

 donald.e.paulk

 d.e.paulk

 d.e.paulk

 depaulk

 spiritandtruthsanctuary

❖

Dr. Burks is available for
Executive Coaching and Training
Writing and Curriculum Development
Speaking Engagements and Event Planning
Corporate Storytelling and Leadership Retreats
Governance Workshops and more!

info@LEADrightToday.com
www.LEADrightToday.com
619-796-6463